BELT AN

'He views B[ ] eco than geopolitical convergence.

BRUNO MAÇÃES

Belt and Road

A Chinese World Order

HURST & COMPANY, LONDON

First published in hardback in the United Kingdom in 2018 by
C. Hurst US & Co. (Publishers) Ltd.,
41 Great Russell Street, London, WC1B 3PL
© Bruno Maçães, 2020
This paperback edition, 2020
All rights reserved.
Printed in the United Kingdom

Distributed in the United States, Canada and Latin America by
Oxford University Press, 198 Madison Avenue, New York, NY 10016,
United States of America.

The right of Bruno Maçães to be identified as the author of
this publication is asserted by him in accordance with the
Copyright, Designs and Patents Act, 1988.

A Cataloguing-in-Publication data record for this book
is available from the British Library.

ISBN: 9781787384071

This book is printed using paper from registered sustainable
and managed sources.

www.hurstpublishers.com

Printed in Great Britain by Bell and Bain Ltd, Glasgow

CONTENTS

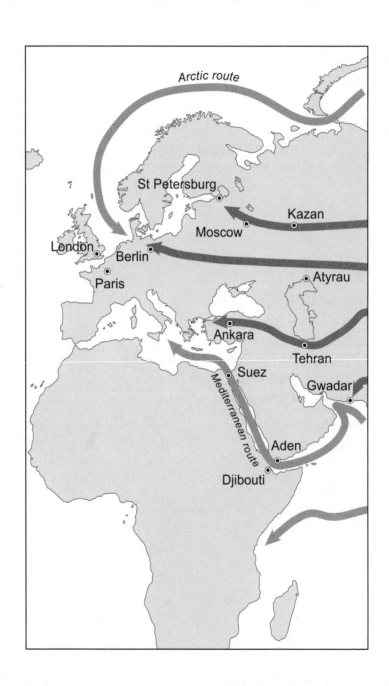

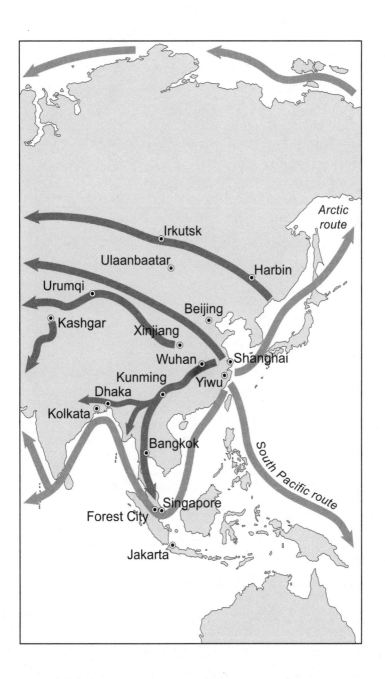

PREFACE TO THE PAPERBACK EDITION (2020)

In January 2020 I spent three weeks traveling in Pakistan, the crown jewel of the Belt and Road, the country where the initiative first took root and therefore the most plausible candidate for the place where its future can be surmised and understood. During my travels I was able to meet with a diverse array of political and economic actors: members of the ruling party, current and retired generals in the military and information services, businessmen and entrepreneurs, as well as a number of influential journalists and activists. In some respects, the visit was a revelation. In others, it helped me confirm some of the main theses I propounded in this book, whose hardback edition was published in December 2018 in the United Kingdom and in 2019 in the United States.

In Pakistan, the Belt and Road is everywhere. A dinner at the Islamabad Club quickly turned into a reminiscence of different visits to China. After a lecture in Lahore, a group of young men and women from Baluchistan wanted to know if the initiative can be defended by anyone who genuinely cares about the future of the region. The acronym for the corridor linking China and Pakistan can be heard in hotel lobbies and restaurants, and it stands out for those who cannot understand Urdu. There are young people who have come of age since the beginning of the initiative and for whom it constitutes the only possible horizon for professional advancement. But there are also a few who hope to reduce its impact and fear for a world where Pakistan has become a Chinese colony. One young woman asked during one of my lectures if the Belt and Road could be considered the new East India Company. More dangerously, an officer in one of the state policymaking bodies wanted me to have a trove of documents showing staggering levels of corruption in Belt and Road contracts. Two projects, the Huaneng Shandong Ruyi Energy and the Port Qasim Electric Power Company Limited, had been overcharged by something like $3 billion. The documents were public, but no newspaper had shown any interest in those facts. I was even able to find out that the infamous Inter-Services Intelligence, the country's top intelligence agency, has a special unit dedicated to collecting critical information about the China-Pakistan Economic Corridor. The political establishment in Pakistan is fully committed to the initiative, but Pakistan's security apparatus has many doubts. That explains why it is still possible to voice public criticisms of the initiative and why security measures continue to hamper its development.

Be that as it may, the Belt and Road has become so central to Pakistani politics that it should not be thought of as a specific project. Rather, it provides the overarching framework for every economic policy and project. In my discussions with economic authorities and think tanks, it quickly became obvious that the main discussion in Pakistan today is about the best way to adapt policy decisions and reforms to the Belt and Road framework. The Belt and Road can thus be compared to the European Union and the role it played for countries in Central and Eastern Europe. What decisions should these countries make in order to better occupy their place within the given political and economic order? Another example of the same process can be found in the history of how countries such as Singapore or South Korea struggled to fit in with the economic paradigm created by economic globalization and global value chains, while benefitting from the opportunities it offered.

My visit thus seemed to return me to the main thesis in this book: the Belt and Road is a political and economic order, not an infrastructure project. During the whole of 2019 I gave more than a hundred talks and speeches on the topic across the five continents. My main message was always that it fundamentally misses the point of the Belt and Road to consider it as an infrastructure project. Even today, that is the most natural way to think about it in the West, something I find deeply perplexing. If we return to the inaugural speech given by Xi Jinping in Astana in 2013, infrastructure is no more than one of the five pillars of the Belt and Road and very obviously not more than an ancillary one. The real action is elsewhere. The initiative is a project of economic and technological development, culminating in a new global political and economic order. Hence the subtitle of my book: *A Chinese World Order*.

When I first became interested in the concept of a Chinese world order, around the time of Xi Jinping's speech in Astana, it was common to hear from different officials and intellectuals in Beijing that the Belt and Road was meant to be completed in 2049, around the time of the first centennial of the new China. Last year, while living in Beijing, I started hearing that the temporal horizon was even longer. Many spoke openly of a hundred-year project. Obviously, these are not infrastructure projects. The Marshall Plan was concluded in just a few years. The Belt and Road aims to create a new political and economic order. Interestingly, it is in Pakistan that this is better understood.

What then is the Belt and Road? As I argue in this book, the best way to answer this question is to directly address what the Belt and Road is for. It will perhaps surprise a Western readership to know that this is a question often discussed in China. In an opinion piece or a lecture by a professor, the message is obviously extracted from the official documents, but there are many contexts where a different opinion may be expressed. I remember a lecture I gave in Wuhan in the summer of 2019. At the end a doctoral student rose to ask a surprising question: "Why do we need the Belt and Road? Why are we sending all these jobs abroad, all this money? We need it here." It was an argument coming from what we in the West would broadly call a populist sensibility. On that occasion, as on many others, I was the one defending the Belt and Road against my Chinese interlocutor.

My argument was that the initiative provides a solution to a major problem that cannot be solved in any other way. As China continues to rise to the pinnacle of the world economy, it faces increasing difficulties and resistance. Some of these difficulties are political, and the Belt and Road does in fact anticipate their development. In some respects, the initiative helped crystallize a more antagonistic position towards China in the United States and India—to a much lesser extent elsewhere—but those developments were inevitable and the Belt and Road tried to address them in advance by putting in place the rudiments of a Chinese-led global economic network.

The difficulties are also economic, and perhaps primarily so. It is common in certain liberal circles to believe that a country can move up in the technological value chain by focusing on domestic reforms and policies. Chinese authorities do not take this approach seriously. They believe in the existence of a global political order. Countries occupy different positions in the existing order. If a country as large as China wants to move closer to the center, it can only hope to do so by implementing a series of changes akin to a revolution. That is the fundamental meaning of the Belt and Road.

In order to become a technological leader, China needs to vastly expand its global presence and influence. There are three main reasons why this is the case. First, the investment in new key technologies is so massive that it can only have an adequate return if access to genuinely global markets is assured. But how can they be assured if powerful competitors will do everything to close them off to Chinese companies? Second, you need access to global value chains and reliable suppliers. If a country wants to move its factors of production to higher segments of the value chain, it needs to ensure a reliable network of suppliers. Third, it needs to transform its own key technologies into global standards—the source of endless streams of revenue in royalties and licensing fees—a process highly dependent on its ability to exercise power within the international bodies responsible for determining what these global standards are.

The brief description above should be enough to show how absurd some common criticisms of the Belt and Road truly are. Among those I have heard: "Why is China spending money on this rather than on its technological development?" "China should be focusing on economic growth." "China should worry about what is happening to Huawei and will happen with its other companies in the future." By now the reader should be quite capable of guessing what the answer to these questions is. The Belt and Road is about China's technological growth. It is about ensuring that the Chinese economy can continue to grow. And it is most definitely a response to the obstacles Huawei has been running into: the disappearance of important markets, the disruption of supply chains and the struggle for the key technologies of the future.

2020   * * *

On January 20, the day President Xi Jinping made his first public statement on the coronavirus, I was crossing the border between Pakistan and India. With me was Venki Ramakrishnan, a biologist and winner of the Nobel Prize in Chemistry in 2009. We had spoken together at a public event in Lahore. The outbreak never came up, not at the event nor in conversation. But it didn't take long for the situation to change.

On January 23, Xi imposed a strict cordon sanitaire on Wuhan and three other cities. Two days later, as I waited in Jaipur for a short flight to Agra, I was joined in the terminal by a crowd of Chinese tourists, all of them heavily masked. One young man wore a giant black elastomeric respirator, looking distinctively cyberpunk. Did he know something we did not?

A week later I was at Indira Gandhi Airport in Delhi, waiting for a flight to Kathmandu. When I reached the security line, the person behind me was none other than Ramakrishnan, whom I had last seen at the Pakistan border ten days earlier. As we placed our bags in trays and layed them on the conveyor belt, he told me that there was nothing to fear. The odds of getting the virus were minimal and the odds of dying from it if you got it were again negligible, he explained.

I waited for Ramakrishnan at the other end of the security check and asked him what he thought the odds were of two people meeting in Pakistan and then by chance running into each other in India ten days later. He laughed.

It is my last memory of laughing about the virus.

What started as a catastrophe for China is shaping up to be a moment of strategic opportunity, a rare turning point in the flow of history. Suddenly, the protests in Hong Kong, carrying a mortal threat to political stability on the mainland, were brought to an abrupt halt. More crucially, the pandemic set in motion a global competition to contain the virus, for which China and the Chinese Communist Party seemed uniquely prepared.

As the virus spread to the whole world, it became apparent that Western societies—Beijing's true rivals—did not have the ability quickly to organize every citizen around a single goal. China, which remains to a large extent a revolutionary society, is

Use This segueway to BRI

critique

a mobilized army capable of dropping everything else and marching in one direction.

Needless to say, the pandemic simultaneously created a number of difficulties for the Belt and Road. They are first of all logistical. Several projects in South and Southeast Asia had to be put on hold after the virus forced Chinese workers and engineers to remain at home in China. Then there are the consequences of the global economic crisis. Loan repayments have quickly become impossible for many developing countries, particularly in Africa. In fact, China announced in June the suspension of debt repayment for seventy-seven developing countries and regions. Beijing will have to adapt to the new facts. Finally, there is the more fundamental point that an initiative aimed at increasing China's global economic power will be considerably more difficult to execute at a time when the public in most countries has turned against globalization, blaming it for the crisis and even the pandemic. "More China" might become a difficult proposition to defend now that many—rightly or wrongly—blame China for the obvious individual and collective distress brought about by Covid-19. Access to dollar-denominated funds, critical to finance Belt and Road projects, will grow increasingly difficult.

On the other hand, the epidemic creates opportunities and these seem much more significant. If one subscribes to my thesis that the Belt and Road is a revolutionary project, then the conclusion is obvious: it is much easier to bring about a revolution during periods of turmoil than during the calm. Even those loan repayment difficulties, so inconvenient at first glance, may well allow China to extract all sorts of political concessions from their troubled economic partners. Mao once said, "Everything under heaven is in utter chaos, the situation is excellent." And so it seems at present, as seen from Beijing.

There are three main levers that China can use to upturn the existing global order. The first is the direct comparison between the situation in China and elsewhere. The numbers of cases and fatalities provided by Chinese authorities probably misrepresent the real figures by more than an order of magnitude, but the fact remains that a semblance of normalcy was achieved in a short period of time and Chinese diplomats stationed all over the world have taken to the media to issue a challenge to America and to compare the chaos in American cities and hospitals with what they see as China's singular success in stopping the epidemic. To the extent that the United States failed to do the same, its prestige will suffer a severe blow. People all over the world will quickly change their perceptions about relative power and capacity.

The second lever resides with industrial value chains. For weeks General Motors, Ford, and Fiat Chrysler closed all their automotive production plants across the United States and Canada. In the meantime, China contained the worst of the pandemic to one province, allowing economic activity to quickly resume elsewhere. The most recent data show renewed activity in the flow of goods across the country, as well as at ports worldwide that do business with China. Growth resumed in the second quarter of 2020, while the United States was faced with a 10% contraction. If the crisis in Europe and America continues for much longer, Chinese companies will be able to dramatically expand market share and replace Western-led value chains. Prepare for a worldwide wave of Chinese acquisitions at knockdown prices. Finally, in a more extreme scenario, important countries could experience the kind of economic shock that leads to widespread social and political collapse. At that point, China would have a unique opportunity to step in, provide aid, and refashion these countries in its own image. A recent agreement with Iran—including new investment projects but also Chinese access to energy and transport infrastructure—may be an early sign of new opportunities.

* * *

PREFACE TO THE PAPERBACK EDITION (2020)

The most revealing visit during my Belt and Road circumnavigation over the last two years was indubitably to Sihanoukville in Cambodia. Few places in the world today capture so perfectly the possibilities of a world in flux. But Sihanoukville is also a certain image of hell.

The town was for many decades a hippie destination for young Europeans in search of sun, drugs and cheap room and board. Some backpackers still arrive today, but it feels like an error based on reading outdated travel guides. Sihanoukville has changed, as my driver from the airport immediately makes clear: he spent many years learning English, but all that has gone to waste because what he needs today is to speak Mandarin.

Sihanoukville is fundamentally a Chinese city, a city with Chinese characteristics. The population has more than doubled, but suddenly Cambodians comprise only about a third of the new total. The signage in shops is either in both Khmer and Chinese or in Chinese only. Locals might find it difficult to navigate a town they can no longer recognize, but that is not their main problem. Prices have skyrocketed, so many are leaving for other regions in Cambodia. It is quite possible to make a fortune selling the family land. Those without property are relegated to driving a rickshaw or finding jobs in cleaning. Even construction workers are Chinese.

The explosive growth of Sihanoukville means that the town was left without the basic city services such as rubbish collection or drainage. During the monsoon, when I visited, the streets are transformed into fast and murky rivers, dragging all the uncollected trash with them. Try to leave your car and you might soon find yourself waist-deep in foul water.

It all started with the deep water port. Chinese companies invested in port projects and a new economic zone aimed at benefitting from the growing transport infrastructure. Back in China, the news traveled fast. While some were making money on infrastructure projects, others spotted different opportunities. With its dollarized economy, Cambodia could offer a unique opportunity for money-laundering. More than a hundred casinos sprouted in Sihanoukville and the real estate market took off. Fortunes were made and at a time when it was becoming increasingly difficult to make them at home in China. Online casinos established themselves in Sihanoukville, bringing workers from China and catering to customers on the mainland, where the business is outlawed. A number of criminal gangs from China are now present in Sihanoukville. They, more than local authorities, set the law. Every now and then, the town witnesses a street shooting. The largest casinos have built their own security forces.

None of this follows a plan or a strategy. The government in Beijing is more wary than proud of what has taken place in Sihanoukville. It has tried to close down the illegal online casinos, a source of distress back in China and a channel for capital flight. If Cambodia allows us to perceive the future direction of the Belt and Road, we should probably close with two main lessons. First, the initiative will leave no stone unturned as it expands all over the globe. Second, it is less a carefully delineated plan than simply the expansive movement of Chinese society— which is now too wealthy, too dynamic and too powerful to be kept within its borders.

Does China have a universal model for the world as a whole? Does China want to shape the world in a certain way? Sihanoukville shows us that the process is rather more organic than one might think at first. As it creates a new order around the Belt and Road, China will create an order that reflects its principles because—even if it does not want the world to become like China—that is the only way it knows how to create order. As the Chinese intellectual Tian Feilong has argued, "China is following a path that the United States took, seizing opportunities, developing outward, creating a new world."[1] It is that world that I attempt to map in my book.

INTRODUCTION

THE GREAT MAP OF MANKIND

When J.R.R. Tolkien was asked by a reader how he had approached the composition of *The Lord of the Rings*, a book that took twelve years to write and spans more than a thousand pages, he answered: "I wisely started with a map and made the story fit." So it is. When imagining new worlds we often start with a map.

For seventy years, our map of world politics was organized in a certain way. The center of global political and economic power came to be located in the United States, from where it radiated to the maritime edges of the large Eurasian supercontinent—a kind of forward deployment against the dangers emanating from its inner core. Western Europe and parts of East Asia were seen as natural extensions of American power, aligned with Washington in values and goals and enjoying significant autonomy from their senior partner. Inevitably, the large landmass of Eurasia remained divided into two areas, according to the path of historical development they had embarked upon: the Western path, to be replicated in countries such as Japan and South Korea, and an alternative path and ideal, defined in different measures and in different ways by Moscow and Beijing, about which there was much less clarity and unity and which sometimes meant little more than the negation of the former.

What took observers by surprise was not that the Eurasian supercontinent emerged from the Cold War as an increasingly integrated space, but that it became so not according to a Western model, but rather as the stage for many different and conflicting political ideas.

The new map of world politics is radically different from the previous one. The United States has seemingly abandoned any pretension to shape the world in its image. American power is still a force to be reckoned with, but from now on it will be exercised at a distance. Just as the United Kingdom in the nineteenth century lived in a precarious relation of distance and proximity to the continent across the Channel, so does the United States appear today as both a part of Eurasian politics and a separate unit enjoying considerable autonomy and independence.

At the same time, new powers have been emerging in Asia that can no longer be seen as pale or imperfect copies of Western society. With the disappearance of the old ideological battle lines and the establishment of new economic links, a new geographic entity started to emerge: Eurasia, the supercontinent extending from Lisbon to Shanghai or even Jakarta. One could argue if this is a return to an older time or the dawn of a new age. The latter would be more exact: romantic images of the Silk Road or Marco Polo's adventures cannot hide the fact that trade along those routes was insignificant and almost no one made the whole journey from sea to sea. As for Genghis Khan, practically limitless as his empire was to become, it quickly broke apart into separate units, prefigurations of future states or empires.

As we list the main centers of influence bringing Eurasia together, pride of place must be given to China and its major geopolitical project, the Belt and Road. In our map it should appear as nine arrows crisscrossing Eurasia in all directions: six economic corridors on land and three sea routes whose final goal is to create a new global economy and place China at its center.

INTRODUCTION

Eurasian trade in goods is now close to $2 trillion each year, consistently more than double the volume of Transatlantic trade and significantly more than Transpacific trade. This is all the more remarkable as this is the axis of the world economy where physical and legal restrictions are most significant and therefore where the potential for growth is the highest. After trade, financial flows will inevitably follow and then cultural and political influence. Whoever is able to build and control the infrastructure linking the two ends of Eurasia will rule the world.

But the Belt and Road is only part of the story. If you want to draw an accurate map of Eurasia you need to add the gradual expansion of Indian power from the Suez Canal to Malacca. Both the Portuguese and the British thought that India encompassed the whole of the Indian Ocean region and this is increasingly how decision-makers in Delhi see the question of India's place in the world. In the next few years we shall see them focused on building a powerful navy and opening military bases in the Horn of Africa and Sumatra, while attempting to integrate the densely populated Indian littoral into its own economic value chains. Raja Mohan, a prominent Indian foreign policy analyst, has argued that "the Indian political and policy establishment, long brought up on the notion that Europe and Asia are different, must adapt to their slow but certain integration into a single geopolitical theatre."

As for Russia, it now looks in four directions at once, a marked improvement upon the double-headed eagle of its state emblem. Traditionally, Russian elites tended to see their task as that of bringing about a gradual but complete integration with a more advanced Europe. That vision is now being replaced by a new self-image: as the center and core of the Eurasian supercontinent, Russia can reach in all directions and provide a bridge between Europe and China on both ends. Vladislav Surkov, a trusted advisor to President Putin, recently argued that Russia is a "Western-Eastern half-breed nation, with its double-headed statehood, hybrid mentality, intercontinental territory and bipolar history." In fact Moscow is also looking south to the Middle East, hoping to acquire control over all the main regions of energy production, and to the north, as global warming transforms the Arctic into an important trade route linking Europe and Asia.

Eurasia is becoming smaller, more integrated, the stage for intense rivalry and competition between different poles, each of them projecting influence outwards and creating new connections. Japan is financing and building infrastructure across the Indian Ocean, all the way to Djibouti, an initiative to which it has dedicated $250 billion. Iran will not rest until it is able to carve a land corridor to the Mediterranean, something it has been deprived of since the Sassanian Shahs 1,400 years ago. Turkey now acts independently of its Western partners and has started to relish the status of a Middle Eastern country, in the process bringing that troubled region to the very borders of the European Union.

Europe has its own strategy too, although it is far from a conscious one. It consists of creating "little Europes" all over the supercontinent: small classes of people in all major metropoles who mimic the European way of life, individualistic and cosmopolitan, connected in tight networks and sharing a similar ethos and common economic and cultural projects. Our map needs to include this spider web of cosmopolitan neighborhoods in Istanbul, Moscow, Mumbai, Shanghai and many other places.

A new world map is being built before our eyes. The new Eurasian century is not one where different regions of the world converge towards a single model. For the first time in many centuries, we are forced to live with cultural contradiction without immediately explaining it away as a result of societies existing at different stages of historical development. But neither is this a world of clear borders and separations. For all their differences, the main political and economic blocs are increasingly integrated. The vast supercontinent stretching from Lisbon to Jakarta is increasingly connected and interdependent, concentrating about two thirds of the world's population and global economic output. Certain regions of the supercontinent are dense areas of technological innovation. Others are enormously rich in natural resources. More importantly, perhaps, it is here that the United States finds the only state actors rivalling it in power and wealth: China, Russia, the European Union, perhaps India in the future, as well as smaller states it nonetheless regards as security threats. Even in the limit case of a world war, it is highly unlikely, if not absurd, that a generalized conflict between, for example, China and the United States could take place in the Pacific. It would be conducted where important allies and enemies can be regimented, where natural resources and large populations exist and where industry is concentrated.

* * *

The Belt and Road is the Chinese plan to build a new world order replacing the US-led international system. If it succeeds, it is very likely that we shall use the name to refer to the new arrangements, much as we use "West" as a shorthand for the existing order. And thus the map of the Belt and Road is already in its fundamental traits the map of the world to come—as China imagines it. What do we see in this map? China is the only country that can genuinely be said to be universal, to overstep its boundaries, extending its presence to distant geographies. This is the clearest marker of a superpower and therefore it is still today a distinctive trait of American power.

The map of the Belt and Road changes that familiar pattern. The United States disappears, having been moved from the obverse to the reverse. Japan, Australia and parts of Western

Europe may want to preserve a privileged relationship with America, but China hopes that it will have enough leverage over them to ensure that those ties are weakened. As for Southeast Asia, the Middle East and Central and Eastern Europe, plans are more ambitious, as China intends to include them in its own orbit. In the new world order, Beijing can project power over two thirds of the world. Other poles of power may retain their sovereignty, but they will be much more regional or even parochial. They will struggle to influence events outside their borders or immediate region. And since China will control a qualified majority of the world economy and global public opinion, any direct confrontation with these other poles—even if they are able to combine—will have a predetermined winner.

The map tells a simple story of power and influence. More than a project or an initiative, the Belt and Road is a movement, representing the slow but ineluctable expansion of Chinese influence. Wherever it finds a vacuum or an area of little resistance, it moves in. Where it finds opposition, it stops, if only momentarily. A colour map is a good representation: check back a few months later and some countries or regions may have changed from their original grey as they join the Belt and Road. The core of the old order—in North America and Western Europe—may one day join as well, but in their case only the symbolic recognition that China is the new global superpower will be in order.

Start with the map and the story will follow. In formal terms it has much in common with a thriller. There is a plan or a plot to take over the world, but everything else is radically uncertain. Chinese leaders muse about their intimation that we have arrived at a critical turn in world history, but the way they approach it is much closer to Lenin than to Marx. Nothing is predetermined, everything is to be decided by the virtue of the participants, their ability to grasp a unique and possibly fleeting opportunity. They would agree with at least the second half of the dictum—common in Europe during the Renaissance—that fortune is a woman whose hair falls over her face so she is hard to recognize and bald at the back so she is hard to grab once she has passed. The United States may yet preserve its dominium for a long time. The existing order may survive if China makes some of the same mistakes it has made in the past.

It is a very human story, full of doubts and hesitations, dreams and fears. Sometimes, as the head of the China Foreign Policy Center of the Central Party School, Luo Jianbo, has said, the feeling is "that everyone is drunk and we are alone, that all nations are in decline and we are rising." But other times, deep doubts seep in. Perhaps China will never overcome its limitations, perhaps the opportunity has already passed. Will Chinese leaders and the Chinese people rise to the occasion? Will they know how to avoid past mistakes and, more importantly, will they recognize the moment of truth, the moment when the fate of the world hangs in the balance? China is approaching the center of the world stage to an extent that is unprecedented, it is approaching the realization of the great rejuvenation of the Chinese people to an extent that is unprecedented, and it has the capacity and confidence to reach this goal to a degree that is unprecedented. How should it act?

Some among the leadership are already dissatisfied with an incremental approach and want to push more forcefully. Others want to keep a cool head and push for a clear understanding of China's development and its place in the world as a necessary precondition for action. To me the debate seems to be an instance of the classical opposition between prudence and courage, the intellectual and the martial virtues.

Graham Allison has made the point that China's rise is a story affecting our individual fates because in the end the question of whether a new world order will be born or the status quo preserved is less important than the question of whether the outcome will be determined peacefully or whether China and America are destined for war. As a rapidly ascending China challenges America's predominance, the two nations risk falling into a deadly trap first identified by the ancient Greek historian Thucydides when he argued that it was the rise of Athens and the fear that this instilled in Sparta that made war inevitable. His history provides a factual record of the choices Pericles and his fellow Athenians made of their own free will. Different choices would have produced different results, a lesson worth keeping in mind as we face a similar danger.

Finally, the story in this book is a universal story in the sense that all dimensions of human life play their part in the course of events. The Belt and Road might even be said to resemble one of those Western classical novels where all the disciplines, all the sciences and all corners of human activity are deliberately included. There will be room in this book for economics and cinema, history and philosophy, high politics and criminal intrigue. There will be short sections on shipping, on the steel industry, on digital technology, on mining and on textiles. The action takes place in different geographies, from Africa to Kazakhstan, from the Indian Ocean to the Mekong Delta, from the Balkans to Mongolia.

This is no accident. The Belt and Road is by design a project meant to encompass the whole world and the totality of human life. No other organized project or idea can rival it in this respect. As Jonathan Hillman has put it, the "Belt and Road is so big it is almost impossible for one person to have mastery of it. Sometimes I wonder if China grasps the whole thing."

Writing this book quickly became a lot more difficult than I expected at first. I hope it has become concurrently more interesting to the reader, who may hope to find in the Belt and Road a comprehensive and coherent view of life in the new century.

1

WHAT IS THE BELT AND ROAD?

In 2015, word started to reach Europe's capital cities that the People's Republic of China had launched an ambitious new initiative, a national project, perhaps in the mould of NASA's Apollo Space Mission. Dubbed 'a new Silk Road', it consisted of a number of railway routes criss-crossing the Central Asian steppes, linking China and Europe. Camels were being replaced by trains, but many quickly pointed out that rail had already been superseded by gigantic container ships as the main means of moving goods around the globe.

If China were seeking to expand and revamp port facilities in the Pacific and Indian Oceans that would make economic sense but would hardly be revolutionary. Conversely, if the real core of the initiative were its land component, and its goal were to replace sea cargo transportation with a new network of roads and railroads across the Central Asian steppes, deserts, and mountains, such a project would indeed be a revolution—but one with no economic viability whatsoever. Rail transportation, even if faster than shipping, will always be significantly more expensive, and few economists believe that transportation bottlenecks are a significant obstacle to the expansion of global trade anyway. As the *Financial Times* put it in 2016, "despite the lofty aspirations, the economic viability of the new Silk Road remains unproven. Industry experts say that all rail transport heading west from China is heavily subsidized by local and regional governments, eager to do their part for the new Silk Road."[1]

Received beyond China through the distorting prism of Silk Road romanticism, what we have come to know as the Belt and Road quickly acquired a considerable mystique. China-watchers wondered what the huge new project might be for, what the official statements were hiding, and why Beijing was launching a giant political initiative whose economic rationale remained at best doubtful. Was it designed as a marketing ploy? Was it about tourism, replacing the Trans-Siberian railway and opening up the cities visited by Marco Polo to the contemporary traveller? Or was it perhaps to be explained according to the arcane tenets of that old discipline, geopolitics? Despite the puzzlement, reactions were predominantly positive. The European Union in particular saw in the initiative something rather similar to its own ideas on connectivity and the beneficial spillover effects of transport infrastructure.

Visiting Beijing that year, I was hearing a different story. At home the initiative was not called the "New Silk Road," but "One Belt, One Road." Its scope was so large that the timeline for its realization had been fixed at more than thirty years, with the first phase of the project to be concluded in 2021 and the project as a whole realized by 2049. No one was that interested in those transcontinental trains, except as marketing opportunities—as the first strategy document for the initiative starkly put it, "we should cultivate the brand of China-Europe freight trains." The measure of its early achievements were rather the industrial parks being launched and the massive ports whose construction or renovation would draw billions in investment.

WHAT IS THE BELT AND ROAD?

An interconnected system of transport, energy and digital infrastructure would gradually develop into industrial clusters and free trade zones and then an economic corridor spanning construction, logistics, energy, manufacturing, agriculture and tourism, culminating in the birth of a large Eurasian common market. Trade, not trains.

Since President Xi Jinping had announced the plans a little less than two years before, everyone had set to work. Books were being published, think tanks devoted to the initiative had been created, course curricula had been redesigned, exhibitions were organized in hundreds of cities and an entrepreneurial soul had created a matchmaking service introducing Ukrainian women to Chinese men "as part of the Belt and Road." The initiative was fast on its way to becoming a household name. It connected old Taoist wisdom with shiny postmodern tech cities, linking past and future in an unbroken chain of historical development. Generals had been put in charge of tactics and strategy. Soldiers and missionaries were being regimented to take the new gospel to the four corners of the earth. The world would never be the same again.

Three more years have passed and the Belt and Road has continued to grow in our imagination. In Europe and the United States it is no longer viewed as a quaint revival of the ancient Silk Road. Discussions of the initiative are now much more often about the future. China has emerged as a threat to a Western rules-based global order and the Belt and Road is now often described as a dagger aimed at the heart of our economies and societies. The German and French governments have—after a period of silence and then apprehension—come out against the project's hegemonic intentions. In the United States, other, more pressing issues remain at the center of the White House's China policy, but in several statements the former Secretary of State Rex Tillerson described the Belt and Road as a Faustian pact by which countries sacrificed their independence for cheap loans. In India a large segment of the foreign policy establishment frets about Chinese encirclement. For many commentators in South and Southeast Asia, the Belt and Road is a project of Chinese expansionism with a thinly disguised military element, as China builds dual-use ports that berth its cargo ships and military vessels, and opens its first overseas bases in places such as Djibouti and—soon enough, surely—Pakistan and Sri Lanka. Tanks, not trains.

In May 2017 China brought together thirty or so national leaders at an inaugural summit devoted to presenting the Belt and Road concept to the wider world. The initiative was promoted abroad via a blitz of television programs and interviews, comprehensive newspaper coverage, music videos and even bedtime stories for children. The Belt and Road was the lead story in most international media outlets and many in Europe and the United States became aware of it for the first time.

Perhaps unsurprisingly, these initial moments of international fame were also marked by a very public display of the difficulties and opposition faced by the project. India announced just one day before the event that it would not be participating, explaining that in its current form the Belt and Road will create unsustainable burdens of debt, while ignoring India's core concerns relating to sovereignty and territorial integrity. Several European countries stated their general support for the initiative, but in a surprising move declined to sign a key trade statement that the Chinese leadership had hoped to produce during the forum. This reluctance was said to stem from concerns over transparency of public procurement—always a priority for the European Union in its external relations—but was also connected to Chinese attempts to increase its influence in parts of Europe.

China is quickly assuming a central role in world politics. Suddenly, every global story has a China angle, whether it is the growing instability in the Balkans, the coup in Zimbabwe, domestic politics in Australia or the midterm elections in the

United States. The traditional opaqueness of Chinese politics and of the Chinese state was once a useful shield, a means of staying out of the limelight. Now it is a way to magnify Beijing's reach: that we know so little about what China is doing seems to show that it is present everywhere. As Howard French puts it in his recent book, East Asia and the Western Pacific are starting to look less and less like a place configured for the needs and ends of the West and, in a return to the past, ever more like the world briefly dominated by China from the late twelfth century until the early sixteenth. China is already the largest trading partner for almost every country in the region and—short of total war with the United States—its military is quickly acquiring superiority across the region.[2]

New clashes, new stories, new mental maps. The world after the Belt and Road will never be the same as it was before. More than any other project, it has come to symbolize a new phase in China's rise, the moment when Beijing embraces its role as a new superpower, capable of remaking the world economy and attracting other countries to its own economic orbit and ideological model. As such, the Belt and Road offers a concrete and vivid introduction to the new China. But its logic and structure are also a natural—almost inevitable—development of the recent trajectory in China's development and cannot be understood in isolation from that context. The Belt and Road did not spring from the earth fully formed, ready to take on the world. It has a history or, better put, a story. That must be the starting point for our exploration.

* * *

As China embarked on its watershed "reform and opening up" under Deng Xiaoping, Chinese foreign policy had to adapt to the new focus on economic development. The possibility—always present with Mao—of a coming war with the Soviet Union or the United States receded from view. Deng's main political achievement was to convince the Chinese Communist Party that the country's national interest now lay in developing peaceful and even friendly relations with the capitalist world. Mao had sought revolution at home and abroad. Deng set his eyes on more earthly goals: making China powerful, prosperous and respected. As he explained in 1978 after Mao died, China had to overcome its reluctance to learn from the developed countries. To achieve the fullest modernization of its economy and society, the Chinese had to draw on inputs of science, technology, managerial skills and physical capital to be found in advanced capitalist economies. This consideration ultimately explains why China's partnership with the United States against the Soviet Union would continue throughout the Cold War and beyond. An entente of sorts— never very deep, but one offering the perpetual promise of future convergence—created a favorable environment for the explosive growth of the Chinese economy during these decades.[3]

At one point in his early efforts to modernize the Chinese economy, Deng had supported the Ministry of Transportation's conclusion that China was not yet up to building large commercial ships and that, in the short run, in order to boost trade, it would have to purchase such vessels overseas. Jiang Qing— Mao's last wife and the leading figure of the Gang of Four—was herself plotting to concentrate power in her own hands and saw an opportunity to weaken Deng, arguing publicly that he was wasting the country's money buying ships and that his actions showed that he had a comprador mentality and worshipped things foreign. Domestic vessels, she wrote, are just as good.[4] The episode offers a good example of the internal resistance Deng was forced to confront and overcome in order to implement an ambitious modernization program. His decision to normalize relations with the United States while Washington continued to sell arms to Taiwan was one of the most difficult and important of his political life, a decision dictated by his long-standing conviction that the only way to speed up China's modernization was to gain access to the West's vast reservoirs of capital and technology. The strategy started to pay off. In 1980 China was admitted to the World Bank and the International Monetary Fund. In the same year, Chinese exports were granted Most Favored Nation status, something that continued to be denied to the Soviet Union and is at the root of the boom in Chinese exports to the United States and, ultimately, the diverging paths taken by China and Russia since that time.

In his 2002 report to the National Congress, General Secretary Jiang Zemin foresaw a "twenty year period of strategic opportunity," during which China would benefit from good relations with the United States, allowing it to concentrate on economic growth and full-scale modernization. During this era, Deng's teaching of "*tao guang yang hui*", or keeping a low profile, remained a guiding principle, but none of the senior figures in China's leadership ever entertained any illusions that such a favorable environment could last forever. China was growing too big and too powerful to avoid raising new suspicions among the major global powers, jealous of their position and naturally unhappy to see a new rival arriving on the scene. Nor could it expect the international political and economic system to continue to satisfy its domestic needs, now that these were becoming increasingly more demanding.[5]

The Belt and Road reflects the change towards a more active foreign policy strategy, one aimed at shaping China's external environment rather than merely adapting to it. It is anchored in the realization that this environment will become more hostile, as the United States once again perceives China a major strategic rival and—perhaps even more decisively—as China's growth and importance in the international system places greater demands on other countries.

By increasing investments abroad, China may hope to find more profitable outlets for its foreign exchange reserves—most of which are in low-interest-bearing American government securities—while creating new markets for Chinese companies. Take the example of steel production in China. Over the last decade, heavy investment in the steel industry led to a severe problem of overcapacity. How could Beijing deal with it? The response favored by Western advisors would be to allow market mechanisms to dictate the fate of the industry's most outdated segments, but this is an outcome the Chinese Communist Party could never countenance. On the one hand, the social impact would adversely affect the main variable of legitimation for the Party: economic and social development. A steep drop in profits, rising debt, bankruptcies and unemployment—overcapacity was quickly becoming a threat to the state's financial and political stability. In 2016 Guangxi Nonferrous Metals Group, the Chinese state-owned metal producer, was declared bankrupt, the first ever issuer in China's interbank bond market to be placed in formal bankruptcy. The company blamed its default on consecutive losses. Steel and nonferrous metals smelters had been among the hardest hit of China's industrial firms following an extended real estate downturn. Its creditors included China Development Bank, Minmetals International Trust Co, Shenwan Hongyuan Securities and Shanghai Pudong Development Bank.

Even if viable, a market-based solution would mean that the main economic decisions would no longer be taken by the state and therefore that the reach of the market would have to be expanded, so that it could be relied upon to steer economic processes. The alternative was obvious. If the domestic market could no longer absorb China's steel production, exports would have to fill the gap. In retrospect, the overcapacity problem was a result of the 2008 global economic crisis. Predominantly affecting Western economies, it reduced demand for Chinese steel. The differential between the West's rates of economic growth and those China needed for its own charted path of economic development was becoming unsustainable. In 2012—the year before the inauguration of the Belt and Road—China's production-to-capacity ratios in iron and steel, cement, aluminum, sheet glass and shipbuilding were 72 per cent, 73.7 per cent, 71.9 per cent, 73.1 per cent and 75 per cent respectively.

Some Chinese commentators speak of China's predicament as having "two heads abroad" ("*liangtou zai haiwai*"). Critically dependent on accessing commodities, energy and raw materials while needing to find constantly growing markets for its exports, China is as deeply integrated in the global economy as the United States or Europe, but it still lacks the tools to project its power abroad.[6] Its situation could be compared to that of Victorian Britain, which was also dependent on imported commodities and export markets. Yet the British had a vast empire and the most powerful navy in the world. Can China develop a functional equivalent?

If the imbalances arise from the dynamics of global interdependence, they can be solved only within the same sphere. But how could this be done at a time when mature markets like the United States or the European Union were also struggling to preserve their steel industries, often by contemplating imposing tariffs against Chinese steel? The realization that China was now highly dependent on foreign markets made it clear that some level of political influence over the latter would have to be developed. European countries in the nineteenth century and then America in the twentieth had been pushed in that direction. China might be forced to do the same.

A watershed moment arrived at the convening of the Working Conference on Neighborhood Policy in October 2013, where President Xi Jinping announced that China should be more proactive in promoting diplomacy with its neighbors, should strive for a sound environment around China, and should make China's

Break of Dug

development more beneficial to neighboring states for purposes of common development. It was a bold break with the deliberate modesty of Deng's foreign policy, a forerunner of sharper breaks to come and a powerful early manifestation of Xi's stature. It was the moment when "striving for achievement" replaced "keeping a low profile" as the fundamental tenet of Chinese foreign policy. The former is appropriate to a rising power, the latter to a weak state, incapable of influencing events outside its borders. Xi argued that "our diplomacy must keep with the times and be more proactive." Guiding other states will replace the policy of "never taking the lead", which is a policy suitable for weak states, or one that signals weakness. That old guideline had been proposed against the background of the collapse of the Soviet Union when many hoped that China would take the lead in the struggle against the capitalist world. It was an appropriate response then, but has lost relevance, given China's new international position.[7] As Xi argued in that programatic speech, "our international objectives are to strive for favorable external conditions for China's reform, development and stability, to safeguard state sovereignty, security and development interests, and to maintain world peace and stability, and promote common development."

Some countries, of course, could be influenced more easily than others. This was particularly the case with developing countries. With their economies still relatively pliable, they could be helped along a path allowing them to fit as seamlessly as possible with Chinese needs. It seemed obvious, to return to our example, that a country could become a major importer of steel only if investment in infrastructure and construction were significantly increased—and Chinese capital could contribute to this. The next few years will see an infrastructure construction boom in Southeast Asia, with Indonesia, Thailand and others having announced ambitious mid-to-long-term plans. Needless to say, Chinese companies enjoy advantages in high-speed railways, highways, ports construction and energy production. According to a study published by the Center for Strategic and International Studies in early 2018, of the contractors working on China-funded transport infrastructure projects in thirty-four Asian and European countries, 89 per cent were Chinese, leaving 11 per cent from elsewhere.

Take another example: fertilizers. China produces too much fertilizer for domestic consumption, but countries such as Vietnam and the Philippines have well-identified needs for a reliable supply of phosphate. This overcapacity can be absorbed at one stroke, to the benefit of all. As He Yafei, vice minister of the Overseas Chinese Affairs Office of the State Council, pointed out in 2014, "one country's overcapacity can meet another country's needs."[8] Huang Libin, an official with the Ministry of Industry and Information Technology, explained: "For us there is overcapacity, but for the countries along the Belt and Road, or for other BRIC nations, they don't have enough and if we shift it out, it will be a win-win situation."

The success of Chinese industry in leading the country's modernization could be expanded to other parts of the world—starting with infrastructure but moving to manufacturing. China would get new markets for its exports, but in due time it could also import at favorable terms those goods which could no longer be profitably produced at home. What is more, by controlling the pace and structure of its investments in developing countries, China could transition much more smoothly to higher-value manufacture and services. In the last stages of its modernization, the country should no longer rely exclusively on Western economies to provide a favorable environment. It had to create that environment by its own actions. This was the initial impetus for the Belt and Road. "Therefore, it symbolizes that China is transforming from a participant to a shaper of globalization, and the situation is changing from one where China opens up to the outside world to one where the world opens itself to China."[9] Overcapacity was less the motivation for the Belt and Road than an example of the fundamental problem the initiative was meant to address: China's dependence on a global system it could not shape or control.

Along a range of different policy issues, decision-makers were coming to the realization that China's problems could not be solved exclusively within its borders. A crucial challenge was the uneven distribution of growth among the different provinces, resulting in large regional economic disparities. The government in Beijing had tried to address these disparities through ambitious development plans focused on the western provinces—Xinjiang above all, with its restive Uyghur population, the source of violent confrontations in 2009 and subsequently—but in the past, development in China had only been successful when combined with access to international markets, so a similar solution for the frontier regions had to be sought in new infrastructure and new trade connections with Central Asia, Pakistan and the Caucasus. Cities such as Urumqi in Xinjiang were after all closer to the borders of Europe than to Beijing or Shanghai.

One of the advantages of working within a framework as vague and ductile as the Belt and Road is that different policies can actually be pursued simultaneously—in apparent violation of the economist Jan Tinbergen's admonition that achieving a given number of desired policy goals requires an equal number of tools. Increasing connectivity across Eurasia can help obviate Xinjiang's economic isolation while boosting demand for Chinese steel and aluminum, but it can also be a way to establish new energy routes linking producers in Central Asia and energy-hungry Chinese cities and factories. Chinese dependence on oil and gas imports will continue to grow in the next two decades. Securing cheap and reliable access to energy sources is therefore a priority for Chinese foreign policy. There are ways to limit its exposure to disruptions in energy flows, and all or almost all of these are served by the vision of and projects included in the Belt and Road.

First, China needs to diversify its energy imports, establishing trade links with all important energy producers. In some cases, this depends on building new gas pipelines or expanding the network of ports and oil terminals sustaining the global oil market. Developing new technology in renewables will also benefit from the Belt and Road. In some cases renewable energy can be more profitably produced abroad through Chinese investment, in others Chinese-produced technology will be exported worldwide. To make the transition to a low-carbon energy system economically viable, China needs to find new markets for its renewables technology and expand markets for civil nuclear technology. Finally, the Belt and Road can be used to develop new trade and energy routes along historically disadvantaged regions, thereby reducing China's vulnerability to an American naval blockade of the Malacca strait in case of conflict.

In 2016 80 per cent of China's imported oil passed through the Indian Ocean and Malacca Strait into the South China Sea. If a maritime crisis or a war were to happen, these routes could be cut off. In 2003 President Hu Jintao noted that "some large countries are continually interfering in and attempting to control shipping through the Malacca Strait." This critical vulnerability has since become known as China's "Malacca Dilemma."[10] It is revealing that those Chinese who criticize the dilemma end up preserving it or even expanding its scope. Mei Xinyu, a researcher at an internal Ministry of Commerce think tank, dismisses the notion of a "Malacca Dilemma" only to replace it with an "Indian Dilemma." He notes that China's vulnerability extends much beyond the Malacca Strait. In that respect its position is much worse than that of Japan in relation to its quasi-enemy during the Cold War, the Soviet Union, which indeed had its eyes on the Strait. Now China's quasi-enemies are the navies of America and its allies. "In order to cut off oil and gas supplies from the gulf to China, they just need to advise Gulf countries to close oil wells, they don't need the Malacca Strait."[11]

In just a few years China will need to import 600 million tons of crude oil and 300 billion cubic meters of natural gas annually. According to some estimates, the different continental corridors envisaged by the Belt and Road—extending to Central Asia, Russia, Iran and the Bay of Bengal—will provide up to 143 million tons of crude oil and 206 billion cubic meters of natural gas—a significant portion of China's projected energy needs. "The priority given by the top leadership to enhanced energy cooperation is underpinned by the assumption that such cooperation is a textbook win-win situation: energy-producing countries are happy to export to the promising Chinese market, while China secures access to diversified sources of supply."[12] At a time when energy producers such as Russia are raising their geopolitical game in the Middle East—hoping to acquire greater control over global energy prices—China cannot be left behind.[13]

The internationalization of the renminbi is another case in point. States are traditionally faced with a dilemma when they have the option to promote their currency's internationalization. In neither West Germany nor Japan was internationalization deliberately pursued. Both countries were happy with their status as economic powerhouses with limited geopolitical ambitions. International use of a currency makes it correspondingly more difficult for national monetary authorities to exert a high level of control over economic variables. At the same time it offers important levers of geopolitical influence: a currency's international status gives the country holding the keys to the printing press an exorbitant power to manipulate the exchange rate, force painful adjustment on other countries, extend financial lifelines or apply financial sanctions. Whether China prefers to maintain full control over domestic economic variables or develop a new tool of geopolitical influence is the question behind the internationalization of the renminbi. *Ch. currency as I = BRI*

Predictably, the Belt and Road is offered as a means to further develop the renminbi as a global trade and investment currency by creating opportunities for its greater use in international transactions, especially those related to energy development and investment in infrastructure. Through the initiative, Chinese companies will make increasing amounts of overseas investment, some of which will be denominated in renminbi, as will most of the fundraising required for the Belt and Road initiative, while encouraging companies to use the currency for cross-border trade and cash management. Moreover the Chinese authorities are actively planning to start paying for imported crude oil in yuan rather than the dollar. Oil is the world's most traded commodity and China the largest importer of crude oil, so the measure will flood international markets with yuan and create spill-over effects in other product payments. Exporters such as Russia will likely support the move, as they share the same desire to break the dollar's global dominance.

* * *

The Belt and Road represents the transformation of China from a regional into a global power. Announcing the initiative in two separate speeches in September and October 2013, President Xi Jinping appealed to the spirit of the ancient Silk Road, the maze of trade routes connecting major civilizations across Europe, Asia and Africa one or two thousand years ago. Referring to a world before European hegemony, the Silk Road could be held up as symbolizing a model of global politics based on cooperation and mutual learning. Less obviously, it contained the seeds of a return to a time when China was the center of the global economy and a technological powerhouse, holding the secrets of silk production and sharp-head, flat-rear high speed junks. By embracing the spirit of the ancient Silk Road, the international community was asked to enter a new age. And thus, from the very start, the Belt and Road was defined as a combination of the old and the new.

The initiative has land and sea components, known respectively as the Silk Road Economic Belt and the Twenty-First-Century Maritime Silk Road. The preferred abbreviation in China for the combined initiative is One Belt, One Road. The preferred English translation is now—simply—Belt and Road, a way to recapture the metaphorical and evocative meaning of the Chinese expression. Even the word "Initiative"—once commonly added to the official name for the Belt and Road—is increasingly seen as redundant. The Belt and Road is certainly not one project. It is an idea, a concept, a process, better captured through a metaphor, not an exact description. It is no coincidence that the initiative had, from the outset, both land and sea components. For centuries China has debated whether it is predominantly a land or a sea power, whether it should become a continental or a maritime nation. The Belt and Road affirms both strategies as equally valid. It could perhaps more appropriately be named— were it not to convey an expansionist slogan—Land and Sea.

The geographic scope of the initiative remains vague and indeterminate. A number of countries have on occasion been included within its central perimeter, but the list was never final or exclusive, and nor was it even confirmed as coming from an official source. The maps circulating today are no less tentative and unofficial. The most commonly used was drafted by Xinhua, a news agency, and its meaning was left rather opaque and confusing: a line undulates from Xian to Istanbul, but no one knows if it is meant to represent a road, a railway or something less material, such as influence or power. By crossing the troubled states of Syria and Iraq, it raises more questions than it answers.[14]

WHAT IS THE BELT AND ROAD?

Recapturing the metaphorical meaning of the original Chinese may help prevent some misunderstandings. It is obvious, for example, that the Belt and Road is meant to include Latin America, the Caribbean and Australia, something that would have sounded very odd if the name of the initiative were—as it once was in the English translation—One Belt, One Road. Chinese decision-makers have no need of being reminded that the world has changed since the days of Genghis Khan and that limiting the Belt and Road to territories along the ancient land and sea Silk Road would be to overlook vital economic regions such as North and South America and most of the African continent. In the first of the two speeches launching the Belt and Road—delivered in Astana, Kazakhstan—Xi Jinping showed no hesitation in attributing the establishment of the ancient Silk Road to China. As he tells the story, during the Han dynasty a Chinese envoy named Zhang Qian was twice sent to Central Asia on missions of peace and friendship. "His journeys opened the door to friendly contacts between China and Central Asian countries, and started the Silk Road linking East and West, Asia and Europe." Standing on the stage of the main auditorium in Nazarbayev University, Xi added: "Today, as I stand here and look back at history, I can almost hear the camel bells echoing in the mountains and see the wisps of smoke rising from the desert, and this gives me a specially good feeling."

Significantly, Xi never describes the initiative he is announcing as a "new Silk Road." That is because the initiative is wholly new—as the scholar Wang Yiwei puts it, China used a very Chinese concept and name "to demonstrate its intellectual property."[15] It is not a trade route but an economic belt: "We should take an innovative approach and jointly build an economic belt along the Silk Road," Xi explained. In Beijing's eyes a Belt is a space of deep economic integration. It may well depend on the development of the necessary transport integration, but it goes much beyond that. In the description presented in Astana, the Belt looks like an extremely ambitious trade agreement organized along five separate dimensions. First, policy coordination, by which Xi means the attempt to find common ground for different national development policies. Second, transport infrastructure. Third, trade, the removal of trade barriers in the countries along the ancient Silk Road. Fourth, currency integration. Fifth, encouraging more intense exchanges and contacts between people.

If the first speech was delivered at the very center of the Eurasian landmass in Kazakhstan, for the second Xi travelled south to the meeting point of the Pacific and Indian Oceans. Nevertheless, the logic of what was proposed was the same. Speaking at the People's Representative Council of Indonesia, Xi argued that Southeast Asia has since ancient times been an important hub along the ancient Maritime Silk Road connecting China to South Asia, the Middle East, Africa and Europe. That should be used as inspiration for the great task of building a Maritime Silk Road fit for the twenty-first century.

The two projects announced in 2013 embraced China's immediate neighborhood and were in that sense a natural starting point. The state of China's relations with the rest of the world finds expression, first and foremost, in the changing relations between China and its neighbors, but one's neighbors have neighbors of their own, so these relations will have to be extended. The Belt and Road is global in nature. Its ruling principle is interdependence, a close network of common interests by which every country's development is affected by the development path in other countries. In his Jakarta speech, Xi called it a "community of shared destiny." The expression featured in Chinese official pronouncements since at least 2007, when it was used to describe relations between Taiwan and the Mainland. Applied to relations outside China's borders, it was a reformulation—a modern version—of the traditional concept of Tianxia (天下), which scholars such as Zhao Tingyang had been popularizing with extraordinary success. Zhao argued that the most important fact about the world today is that it has not become a zone of political unity, but remains a Hobbesian stage of chaos, conflict, noncooperation and anarchy.[16] Looking for a way to frame new political concepts distinct from Western ideas of world order, the Chinese authorities quickly appropriated Tianxia—a notion that originated about three thousand years ago—and made it the cornerstone of their most ambitious geopolitical initiative. The idea of a community of shared destiny and the Belt and Road develop the two sides of every human action. Both have their own emphasis: the former belongs to the idea, the concept or type, the latter is aimed at practice. Together they form the "dialectical unity of theory and practice, goals and paths, value rationality and instrumental rationality."[17]

The general principle of Tianxia—which literally means All-under-Heaven or World—is that relations between units or actors determine the obligations corresponding to their network ties. Relations are based on mutual benefit—or win-win in common parlance—and once established they should take precedence over individual choices. The Western mode of association, which presumes the autonomy of individual units and consists of clear boundaries between the Self and the Other, is excluded. No entity can think of itself in isolation. They exist in Xi's community of shared destiny, from which—and contrary to the dreams of Western political thought—it is impossible to escape. The Belt and Road takes this notion on board by defending that China's problems and challenges cannot be addressed in isolation but only in mutually beneficial relations with other countries. As Xi put it in his speech at the Boao Forum for Asia in 2015, "only through win-win cooperation can we make big and sustainable achievements that are beneficial to all. The old mindset of zero-sum game should give way to a new approach of win-win and

all-win cooperation. The interests of others must be accommo-
dated while pursuing one's own interests, and common development must be promoted while seeking one's own development."

It is a remarkable, even a stunning development in Chinese
foreign policy. Beijing had recognized the benefits of economic
globalization for some time, but until Xi it remained consistently
suspicious of its political and cultural dimensions. Now China
has started to see interdependence as an opportunity. Rather
than advocating the creation of new barriers, it welcomes a vision
of the world where political and cultural influence is allowed to
flow outside national borders. The Belt and Road goes so far as
to advocate innovative forms of economic policy coordination, an
area where, for example, the European Union has made limited
progress. China also plans to set up a new international court for
settling disputes among companies participating in the Belt and
Road. The new Belt and Road dispute settlement mechanism is
aimed at protecting both Chinese and foreign parties' legal rights
and interests, and creating a stable, fair, transparent business
environment governed by the rule of law. It will be comprised of
three international commercial courts. The court in Xian will
deal with commercial disputes along the Silk Road Economic
Belt. The Shenzhen court will cover cases arising along the 21st
Maritime Silk Road. The headquarters of the Belt and Road
court will be based in Beijing.[18]

A new political confidence inspires dreams of infusing the
global order with Chinese values, simultaneously reducing fears
of Western cultural imperialism. Tentatively, China has started
to experiment with its new role, that of a global superpower. It
is much less afraid of political and cultural globalization because
it now believes they can be shaped according to a Chinese
model.[19] The report to the 18th National Congress of the CPC
in November 2012 argued: "In promoting mutually beneficial
cooperation, we should raise awareness about human beings

sharing a community of common destiny. A country should accommodate the legitimate concerns of others when pursuing its own interests; and it should promote common development of all countries when advancing its own development." Since then the concept has become increasingly central to Chinese foreign policy, culminating in the report to the 19th National Congress delivered by Xi Jinping on October 18, 2017, where it became an important part of the Thought on Socialism with Chinese Characteristics for a New Era. On February 10, 2017, the proposition to build a Community of Shared Future for Mankind was first made part of a United Nations resolution. On March 11, 2017, the same proposition was included in a UN Security Council resolution; and on September 11, 2017, the proposition's underlying principle of achieving shared growth through discussion and collaboration was incorporated in the UN General Assembly resolution on global governance.

If we compare the Belt and Road to the most significant contemporary example of cooperation between states—the European Union—it appears as simultaneously less and more ambitious. It is less ambitious because no body of supranational institutions has been envisioned, but it is more ambitious because it touches the core of national sovereignty by propounding a model of state relations where every decision is in principle open to external influence. National sovereignty is never renounced, but neither is it affirmed or consecrated. Tianxia is neither national nor supranational. J.Ch.Sea?

* * *

So what is the Belt and Road? It is a name and little more than a name, but one whose most obvious advantage is that it brings together a number of new, highly significant developments: China's growing international clout, its need to reshape the international economic system in its image and the growing reactions and responses to that project. Past equivalents to the Belt and Road would have to be just as shapeless and ambitious. Perhaps concepts such as "the West" come the closest—even in the manner that a metaphor came to acquire epochal significance. As the scholar Ming Hao dramatically writes, the world does not move from harmony to conflict but from conflict to harmony—from the West to the Belt and Road.[20]

The Chinese authorities are sanguine about the idea of a world system articulating the relations of economic power and dependence at the heart of the global economy. Patterns of specialization and comparative advantage determine the place each country assumes in the global economy and, as a result, the levels of absolute and relative prosperity it may hope to achieve. The global economy is less a level playing field than an organized system in which some countries occupy privileged positions and others, such as China, try to rise to these commanding heights.

It was always like that, as you will be told in Beijing. The difference is that now someone else is inching closer to the center. The Belt and Road is the name for a global order infused with Chinese political principles and placing China at its heart. In economic terms this means that China will be organizing and leading an increasing share of global supply chains, reserving for itself the most valuable segments of production and creating strong links of collaboration and infrastructure with other countries, whose main role in the system will be to occupy lower value segments. Politically, Beijing hopes to put in place the same kind of feedback mechanism that the West has benefited from: deeper links of investment, infrastructure and trade can be used as leverage to shape relations with other countries even more in its favor. The process feeds on itself. Until recently, it seemed that China's growing influence would be contained to its own peripheries. That countries such as Greece and Hungary now openly defend Chinese positions during important meetings in Brussels has been a rude awakening.

WHAT IS THE BELT AND ROAD?

It is the case that the Belt and Road was from the outset defined as a radically new order. In this sense it owes some debt to Mao's revolutionary legacy, as much as to Deng's vision of a world organized as a network of production chains. A corpus of political literature surrounding the Belt and Road seeks to demonstrate that China will be a great power, entirely different from, and morally superior to, recent Western historical examples and that it will usher the whole world towards a new historical age. As the influential geopolitical thinker Wang Jisi notes, "That is a far cry from a global proletariat revolution, but it leaves room for selective opposition to the status quo."[21] In contrast with a West which is described as exploitative and aggressive, China is portrayed by Chinese scholars as inherently benevolent and peaceful. As we have seen already, the Belt and Road is meant to introduce a new theory of international relations that "resolutely rejects" power politics and is committed to settling disputes through dialogue rather than confrontation. These principles are a reformulation of Tianxia, often going so far as propounding old Confucian virtues of "sincerity," "honesty" and "amity" as governing principles for world politics. The Western system of alliances, for example, is often described by Chinese authors as a "tiny circle of friends" leaving everyone else excluded. This language sounds foreign to Western ears, used since Machiavelli to exclude morality from foreign policy and often from domestic politics too. They are a reminder that it would be a mistake to think that China's rise means that the country will occupy the center in a global system remaining essentially the same.

It is true—we have seen it above—that there is a very long tradition of Chinese reflection on world affairs which is different from the Western one. The whole tradition of Tianxia differs from the tradition of political thought going back to the Greeks—the polis as a self-sufficient whole—and later Machiavelli, which is much more interested in questions of sovereignty and conflict. But to note this is not yet to settle the question of the validity of Tianxia as a way to think about world politics. It may transpire that, even though China does not intend the Belt and Road as a geopolitical project, as a project of state rivalry, it may ultimately function in this manner, against China's wishes. *Be Real.*

In this book we shall be looking at some examples that indicate the usefulness of a geopolitical approach to the Belt and Road. Another possibility is to think this is all simply a grand deception, that the Chinese know very well that the initiative is about hegemony and power, but that they simply try to disguise the fact because—as Machiavelli teaches—your rise to power works better if you conceal it from everyone else. Significantly, this interpretation is now quite widespread in the public debate. President Xi felt forced to address it at the Boao Forum in April 2018, where he argued that "the Belt and Road is not a plot of China, but a plan in sunshine." Was the denial also a part of the plot?

The trope of a hidden geopolitical agenda has a long history in analyses of Chinese foreign policy. Most Western observers translate Deng's famous phrase ("*taoguang yanghui*") as "hiding capacities and biding time" or, in other words, building one's capacities in darkness and waiting for the right moment to seek revenge. If the policy articulated by Deng was meant to reduce suspicion of Chinese intentions in other countries, its articulation produced the opposite effect. General Xiong Guangkai, former deputy chief of staff of the PLA, went so far as to write an article discussing how the English version had a negative impact on Chinese foreign policy and recommending alternative translations. It cannot be denied that the term, however translated, connotes trickery and conspiracy in traditional Chinese culture.[22]

And yet the "paranoid style" applied to Chinese foreign policy omits most of what is new and interesting about the Belt and Road. Politics is to some extent always about deception, but to reduce the Belt and Road to a Machiavellian ruse is to overlook the larger forces explaining it and the rich consequences the initiative will have for the normative elements of world order. Already with the notion of a "harmonious world" introduced by President Hu Jintao in 2005, it was difficult or impossible to reduce its meaning simply to propaganda. It was an ideal concept—thus existing at some distance from everyday politics—but that did not mean it was not taken seriously and often firmly defended by public intellectuals and officials.

The Chinese authorities are obviously right that a win-win solution is always possible in the sense that cooperation between two or more states can leave both better off. Where the model breaks down is at the level of different political concepts because these are always defined in opposition to one another. The ideological question—as opposed to the economic one—is inevitably zero-sum because to accept a certain way to organize social relations is to discard different concepts and principles. The fact is recognized by those Chinese scholars who have looked closely at the political implications of the new theory of Tianxia. Xu Jin and Guo Chu take a materialistic approach to the concept of a "community of shared destiny," noting that in Chinese "fate" refers to the life fortunes of life and death, wealth and poverty. Just as in social life one cannot talk about fate without mentioning life and death, in international relations it is not possible to talk about fate without mentioning the happiness and misfortune of nations, their rise and fall, their security and prosperity. Like life and death, these are common to every nation, but the authors do not thereby conclude that the concept of fate is universal in a strict sense. The fate community, they argue, is a community promoted by China. It must reflect Chinese characteristics and highlight China's role as the "master of fate." Someone has to be in charge of making sure that things turn out well. "Each order or system reflects the characteristics and goals of its main advocates and promoters. Therefore in the cause of advocating and promoting the concept of fate community, China must be brave enough to work hard and be rewarded."[23]

Machiavellian politics is the wrong way to look at the Belt and Road, but even if one thinks in more traditional Chinese terms, that does not mean that they will be benign or acceptable to many parts of the world—including the West—because the traditional model is a model of dependency, one in which the center is in China, surrounded by different dependent peripheries—a model of Confucian society that is based on gratitude, and dependency, and respect for those that are more powerful. This is obviously antithetical to Western values. So even if China is eschewing a Machiavellian strategy in favour of some kind of Confucian strategy, applied to world politics, does this mean that everyone must welcome the revolution? What for China might be seen as the beginning of a new age in the history of mankind—predicated on relations of cooperation rather than conflict—will assume rather different hues elsewhere. This would be a system which many parts of the world, and above all the West, could not accept.

In the past Tianxia took a specific legal and institutional form: the tributary system. Under this hierarchical order, foreign states, attracted by the splendor of Chinese civilization, voluntarily submitted to the Chinese court and became vassals, periodically sending embassies to pay tribute to the Chinese emperor. The system was a means of endowing the entire known world with a single political order. It was achieved by singling out a central state responsible for creating and maintaining order under the direct supervision of the highest deity, namely Heaven. Its ruler was the son of Heaven, whose authority alone could surpass territorial borders and bring the whole world together. Instead of territorial boundaries, relations between states were expressed by the aforementioned hierarchical relationship between the center,

China, and the peripheries. The existence of fully independent states would have been contrary to the very idea of Tianxia.

In court meetings, tributary envoys performed certain rituals including the full kowtow—kneeling three times, each time tapping their head to the ground for another three times, for a total of nine taps. The ambiguity of the system—its units were simultaneously part of a single order and left alone to govern their affairs—meant that ritual and symbol became more important than legal status. That element of Tianxia would in our time be represented by economic relations. Legally and politically, the states included in the Belt and Road would remain fully sovereign and independent. In practice, economic power would bind the system together and prevent it from falling apart. It is precisely in this informality that the initiative most obviously differs from the existing Western order which emphasizes legal and institutionalized procedures. The Belt and Road is not an entity with fixed rules; rather, it is deliberately intended to be informal, unstructured and opaque.

An obvious fear for many participants and observers is that the Belt and Road will reintroduce the former hierarchy of the tributary system, even though nothing in the initiative is explicitly intended as a return to that model. Its antiquated rituals and formal procedures lie at the antipodes of the fast-changing and fast-moving China of our days, whose origins are in any case to be found in the fierce repudiation of the imperial system. But the Belt and Road is about interdependence. It aims to bring different states together in the realization of common projects. Because it is based on relations of dependence, it cannot but reproduce relations of power. Some states will be more dependent on China than China is on them.

A moralized notion of international politics will mean that values such as loyalty, gratitude and friendship can easily translate into relations of dependency, especially in a situation where reprisals for charting an independent path are part of Chinese foreign policy. In December 2016, for example, China closed a key border-crossing with Mongolia a week after the Tibetan spiritual leader, the Dalai Lama, visited the country. Hundreds of truck drivers for the mining conglomerate Rio Tinto were stuck at the Gants Mod crossing in south-eastern Mongolia in freezing temperatures. In response to the sanctions, the Mongolian government was forced to issue a number of ambiguous public statements, designed to be spun as a Dalai Lama ban, while letting Mongolia itself interpret it as a simple belief that local organizations would no longer invite him in the future.

As China's economy grows in strength, its overseas lending and investment as part of initiatives such as the Belt and Road will give it further potential for economic leverage. Once a project is under way, China may be able to defer loan disbursements or seek early repayment of loans as a coercive economic tool. After the completion of the project, a Chinese company operating a port might modestly slow transit to send a coercive signal about China's control over a target country's trade flows.[24]

The idea of a "harmonious world" or a "community of shared destiny" may appeal to the pursuit of peace, cooperation and respect for cultural difference, but when—in a curious imitation of the Western concept of the end of history—it is presented as the inevitable endpoint of historical development, it becomes uncompromising and oppressive. Once a "community of shared destiny" has been advanced as the only correct option, the temptation is to start identifying disharmonious elements, those who, as the Chinese authorities like to put it, still harbor a Cold War mentality or a zero-sum approach to world politics. The implication is that the same Chinese elites who developed the concepts guiding the Belt and Road must now be left to decide how those concepts are to be executed. "If everyone behaves harmoniously, an end-state can be imagined where everyone complies with, or is co-opted by, the Chinese elite's notion of what is an advanced culture and a 'win-win' solution: a harmonious world."[25] Participants in the Belt and Road are thus pushed to a position where only two options are possible: agreeing to its basic tenets and goals or declaring oneself on the wrong side of history.

2

NUTS AND BOLTS

The Silk Road Economic Belt and the 21st Century Maritime Silk Road were officially endorsed by the Chinese Communist Party soon after Xi's speeches in Astana and Jakarta—first at the forum on China's periphery diplomacy in October 2013, then by the Third Plenum of the 18th Party Central Committee in November. Work on delineating Xi's vision in detail could start in earnest, but it was not until 2015 that the Belt and Road started to feature in the State Council's reports on government work and in strategy and planning documents.

In February 2015 a new Advancing the Development of the One Belt, One Road Leading Group was established. Its composition provided useful insight into the leadership's concept of the initiative. Chairing the group was first-ranked Vice Premier Zhang Gaoli, a member of the elite Politburo Standing Committee who held primary responsibility for finance, reform and development, and the environment. The group had four vice-chairmen: third-ranked Vice Premier Wang Yang, responsible for the US-China Strategic and Economic Dialogue, Yang Jiechi, a state councilor and former minister of foreign affairs,

Yang Jing, secretary general of the State Council, and last but not least, Wang Huning, the philosopher-king behind Xi, arguably the intellectual creator of the Belt and Road, who was to be elevated to the Politburo Standing Committee in 2017. It is only in unusual circumstances, especially in times of foundings, crises and transitions, that political thinkers can come to exercise such authority. That Wang's counsel has played a critical role since he was recruited by President Jiang Zemin in 1995 suggests there are profound questions confronting contemporary China that are not simply technical or bureaucratic.[1]

On March 8, 2015 Foreign Minister Wang Yi dismissed comparisons of the initiative to the US-sponsored Marshall Plan. For one, the Belt and Road was meant to usher in a new model of international relations, not to salvage or reconstruct a crumbling European civilization. Second, it would be "the product of inclusive cooperation, not a tool of geopolitics, and must not be viewed with an outdated Cold War mentality," Wang said, adding that China's diplomacy in 2015 would focus on making progress on the Belt and Road. Building its own space and area of influence is the path to becoming a world power. China's principal advantages are in the economic domain. Thus the Belt and Road is mainly about economic cooperation, including building factories, roads, bridges, ports, airports and other infrastructure as well as electric power grids, telecommunications networks, oil and natural gas pipelines and related projects.

On March 28, 2015, the National Development and Reform Commission, the Ministry of Foreign Affairs and Ministry of Commerce—the authorship reflects the initiative's double head, designed to stimulate and better integrate China's domestic economy as well as enhance Beijing's influence abroad—released the Vision and Actions on Jointly Building Silk Road Economic Belt and 21st Century Maritime Silk Road, the master plan setting forth guiding principles, main routes and projects, and areas of cooperation for the Belt and Road. In May 2015 Chinese media reported that there were over 900 major projects at the national level already in the pipeline, of which fifty would be launched soon and twenty related to the Maritime Silk Road. The initiative also featured in China's 13th five-year plan, which outlines the country's key priorities for 2016–20 and dedicates a chapter to the aim of moving forward with the Belt and Road.

Finally, in October 2017 the Belt and Road was included in the Chinese Communist Party's Constitution, an entirely unprecedented honor for a foreign policy or infrastructure initiative, ensuring that it will become a core principle, impossible to abandon—and likely to impose on foreign states a corresponding obligation to engage with the Belt and Road if they want to engage with China. Direct attacks on the constitutional principles of other countries are, after all, hardly compatible with diplomatic practice.

* * *

The Vision and Actions document describes the initiative "to jointly build the Belt and Road" as "aimed at promoting orderly and free flow of economic factors, highly efficient allocation of resources and deep integration of markets." Simultaneously, it encourages "the countries along the Belt and Road to achieve economic policy coordination and carry out broader and more in-depth regional cooperation of higher standards." Already in this initial programmatic statement the roles of market and state appear combined. Interestingly, the same dual nature is revealed in the maps of the initiative released at about the same time by Xinhua and other Chinese media outlets. The metropolitan dots connected by lines—market integration—are inscribed not against a plain white background, but typically by superimposing that illustration of market networks on a standard map of national territories. Visually, as a shrewd paper by the scholars Nordin and Weissmann puts it, "the two imaginaries clearly coexist."[2]

The initiative will abide by market rules and international norms, give play to the decisive role of the market in resource allocation and the primary role of the private sector, while letting governments perform their due functions. The list of government functions is suitably vast and wide. Many of the countries included in the initiative are still developing and their economies need massive amounts of infrastructure investment, not easily undertaken by ordinary private enterprises. The Chinese model being exported along the routes of the Belt and Road is in any case one where the state retains control over sectors that are considered strategic, and oversees the way in which the Chinese economy relates to global markets. Governments "need to improve the region's infrastructure, and put in place a secure and efficient network of land, sea and air passages, lifting their connectivity to a higher level; further enhance trade and investment facilitation, establish a network of free trade areas that meet high standards, maintain closer economic ties, and deepen political trust; enhance cultural exchanges; encourage different civilizations to learn from each other and flourish together; and promote mutual understanding, peace and friendship among people of all countries." Internationalization of the kind advocated by the Belt and Road may have a synergetic relation with the preservation and growth of large state-owned enterprises which can engage in long-term investment abroad without being excessively concerned with the next quarter or with stock prices—and only under such favorable conditions ensure their own viability as world leaders. Revealingly, the launch of the Belt and Road was accompanied by a process of merger and acquisitions enabling the creation of truly massive industrial conglomerates. Some authors go so far as to claim that the Belt and Road "represents a grandiose reaffirmation of the

Chinese commitment to state capitalism and its associated power relations."[3]

Connectivity (*wu tong*) projects are seen as a tool in the service of larger goals: "The connectivity projects of the Initiative will help align and coordinate the development strategies of the countries along the Belt and Road, tap market potential in this region, promote investment and consumption, create demands and job opportunities, enhance people-to-people and cultural exchanges, and mutual learning among the peoples of the relevant countries, and enable them to understand, trust and respect each other and live in harmony, peace and prosperity." Cooperation in infrastructure development could be a first step in facilitating the growth of trade, investment and economic development in China and participant countries, but it would also require policy cooperation and domestic efforts to lower trade and investment barriers. The geographic space being transformed must be connected before it can start to grow areas of economic activity; industrial parks along infrastructure routes are slowly integrated to establish regional value chains and eventually support fully developed cities—culturally creative, internationally connected and technologically advanced.

Connectivity is not only or even primarily about roads and railways. Several projects are aimed at building telecommunication networks between Asia and Europe under the Belt and Road and create what the Chinese authorities call a "digital silk road" or a "community of shared destiny in cyberspace." Xi Jinping himself has shown a strong interest in the concept. Inmarsat, a leader in providing mobile satellite services, was the only British company he visited during his state visit to London in October 2015. Around the same time, China and the European Union issued a declaration on the development of 5G mobile networks. The mobile technology is so important that it was highlighted in the Government Work Report delivered by

Premier Li Keqiang during the National People's Congress session in March 2017 and a report by the China Academy of Information and Communications Technology predicted that 5G will drive 6.3 trillion yuan of economic output in the country by 2030. Massive overseas investment fits with China's ambition to boost key technologies in artificial intelligence, big data, smart cities, the industrial internet and cloud computing. An early benefit will come from new opportunities for its e-commerce companies. Many of the Belt and Road countries are yet to experience a thriving e-commerce sector due to a lack of good digital infrastructure. Partly as a result of the initiative, Chinese online retail giants such as Alibaba will be spearheading the development of a truly global e-commerce market.

Data flows will be managed on a global scale and large pools of data connected through new infrastructure and technological breakthroughs. In March 2018, the Guangzhou startup CloudWalk Technology signed a strategic partnership with the Zimbabwean government to begin a large-scale facial recognition program throughout the country. The agreement, part of the Belt and Road, will see the technology primarily used in security and law enforcement and will likely be expanded to other public programs. The project will help the government build a smart financial service network as well as introduce intelligent security applications at airports, railway stations and bus stations. In the process, Zimbabwe may be giving away valuable data as Chinese AI technologists stand to benefit from access to a database of millions of Zimbabwean faces. Rolling out the technology in a majority black population will allow CloudWalk to expand the algorithm's training and to eliminate racial biases, getting ahead of US and European developers. As one commentator put it, this could very well be the latest example of Africa handing over natural resources to China.[4]

The Belt and Road will enable China to further expand and deepen its opening-up, and to strengthen mutually beneficial cooperation with countries in Asia, Europe and Africa and the rest of the world. "It will integrate itself deeper into the world economic system," as the Vision and Actions document puts it, but a grand bargain is presupposed: this new and deeper pattern of opening-up should go with a greater global role for China, as it starts to shoulder more responsibilities and obligations within its capabilities, and makes greater contributions to the peace and development of mankind. Revealingly, the geographic range of the initiative is limited to the Asian, European and African continents—but "not limited to the area of the ancient Silk Road." Its historical mission is explicitly that of reinventing Eurasia as an integrated supercontinent: "The Belt and Road runs through the continents of Asia, Europe and Africa, connecting the vibrant East Asia economic circle at one end and the developed European economic circle at the other, and encompassing countries with huge potential for economic development."

In line with the philosophical notion of a "community of shared destiny" underpinning the initiative, the Belt and Road seeks mutual benefit. It accommodates the interests and concerns of all parties involved, and "seeks a conjunction of interests and the biggest common denominator for cooperation so as to give full play to the wisdom and creativity, strengths and potentials of all parties." The language is that of a dialogue of civilizations— the "Silk Road spirit"—while also appealing to economic theories of comparative advantage. The different countries along the Belt and Road are said to "have their own resource advantages and their economies are mutually complementary." But the ties that bind are first and foremost financial.

The Asian Development Bank has estimated that Asia and the Pacific will require on average $1.7 trillion per year of additional infrastructure investment—or $26 trillion by 2030—if current economic growth rates are to be sustained. This funding deficit amounts to 2.5 per cent of the region's GDP—a full 5 per cent if you remove China from the equation. According to various estimates, the Belt and Road alone would require $4 trillion to $8 trillion to realize its goals. The question, of course, is who will foot the bill?

The terms of Chinese credit to countries along the Belt and Road vary widely, from interest-free loans and even grants in the case of some Pakistan projects to a fully commercial rate in the case of the Ethiopia-Djibouti railway. Revealingly, Djibouti's public external debt has increased from 50 to 85 per cent of GDP since 2015, the highest of any low-income country. Much of the debt consists of government-guaranteed public enterprise debt and is owed to the China Export-Import Bank. China has provided nearly $1.4 billion of funding for Djibouti's major investment projects.

Foreign direct investment and concessional loans make up the vast majority of Belt and Road financing. The former carries far fewer risks for the recipient country, but even in this case they are present. Pakistan, for example, is expected to assume indirect liability for payment of electricity generation projects, which are private-sector investments, with the Finance Ministry obligated to create a revolving fund equal to 22 per cent of the monthly invoicing for electricity projects to ensure seamless repayment of Chinese power producers. Pakistan would also have to bear the burden of paying Chinese companies for electricity that Pakistani distribution companies would not be able to pay for. The chief economist of Pakistan's Planning Commission, Nadeem Javaid, said in 2018 that debt repayment and repatriation of profits would range from $1.5 to $1.9 billion beginning in 2019, to double that in 2020, and peak at $5 billion in 2022. The Chinese company operating the port of Gwadar reportedly receives 91 per cent of the port's profits.

In December 2017 Sri Lanka formally handed control of Hambantota port to China in exchange for writing down the country's debt. Under a $1.1 billion deal, Chinese firms now hold a 70 per cent stake in the port and a 99-year lease agreement to operate it. The $1.3 billion port project was intended to transform a small fishing town into a major shipping hub. In pursuit of that dream, Sri Lanka relied on loans from a Chinese state-owned bank, but the government struggled to repay the debt, with the project incurring heavy losses. The first phase of the Hambantota port project was a $307 million loan at 6.3 per cent interest, much above the typical rates charged for large infrastructure projects. Could anyone have expected a different result from that announced in 2017, almost ten years after construction started? "With this agreement we have started to pay back the loans," Sri Lankan prime minster Ranil Wickremesinghe said during a handing-over ceremony in parliament. China's official news agency tweeted triumphantly, "Another milestone along the path of the Belt and Road." In July 2018, the Sri Lanka government decided to move a naval unit to Hambantota. With reports in the media that China is considering gifting a frigate to the Sri Lankan Navy—the move creates the grounds for the insertion of Chinese training and support teams in Sri Lanka's naval command—it seems clear that a process for the creation of a Chinese naval outpost in Hambantota has begun.

In April 2018, Li Ruogu, the former president of the Export-Import Bank of China, argued publicly that most of the countries along the routes of the Belt and Road did not have the money to pay for the projects with which they were involved. Many are already heavily in debt and need sustainable finance and private investment, he said, adding that the countries' average liability and debt ratios had reached 35 and 126 per cent, respectively, far above the globally recognized warning lines.

* * *

One of the apparent contradictions contained in the Belt and Road is the way it is meant to combine market mechanisms benefiting from comparative advantage and the free flow of economic factors with an active role for the state in providing a common framework for the initiative. Finance is how China attempts to solve the contradiction.

While Western commentators like to speak of the costs and mechanisms for funding the Belt and Road as an external variable, Beijing regards financing mechanisms as a critical part of the initiative, the motor of the engine which gives the Belt and Road a certain pace and direction, bringing its disparate elements together in a coherent whole. The giant state banks—Industrial and Commercial Bank of China, Agricultural Bank of China, Bank of China and China Construction Bank—will retain a dominant role, but new financial institutions have also been created.

The Asian Infrastructure Investment Bank, founded on December 25, 2015 with its headquarters in Beijing and an authorized capital of $100 billion—about half that of the World Bank—considers Belt and Road projects as one of its investment priorities. Thus, it approved $509 million in investments for its first four projects on June 25, 2016, on power, transportation, urban development and other projects in Bangladesh, Indonesia, Pakistan and Tajikistan, all countries along the core area of the Belt and Road.

The Silk Road Fund is a development and investment fund established in Beijing on December 29, 2014 with an investment of $40 billion from the State Administration of Foreign Exchange, China Investment Corporation, Export-Import Bank of China and China Development Bank, focusing on investment opportunities and providing investment and financing support under the framework of the Belt and Road. By June 2016, it had announced three sets of investment projects: to inject capital in the China Three Gorges Corp to develop hydropower plants in Pakistan and other South Asian countries; to fund ChemChina in its acquisition of Italian tyre-maker Pirelli; and to make investments in the Russia-based Yamal LNG project.

Domestic policy banks serve as the backbone for financial cooperation. Quickly following the detailed plans set out in the Vision and Actions document, China Development Bank set up a Belt and Road project pool involving over 900 projects from over sixty countries in transportation, energy, resources and other sectors. In January 2018, Hu Huaibang, chairman of the bank, told a panel at the Asian Financial Forum in Hong Kong that the bank had extended $110 billion in loans to projects along the ancient trade route by the end of 2017 and announced plans to invest an additional $250 billion. The Chinese bank, which has assets of $2.4 trillion, was set up to provide medium- to long-term loans to the country's major economic and social development projects. The bank falls under the direct leadership of the country's State Council and is financially backed by the Ministry of Finance and Central Huijin Investment, China's largest investment company. Similarly, the Export-Import Bank of China started to redirect its focus to Belt and Road countries in 2015. It reportedly planned to finance more than one thousand projects in forty-nine countries, covering transportation, electricity, resources, telecommunication, and industrial parks, and has set up three cooperation funds for investment in the Belt and Road.[5]

Reflecting the planned nature of the Chinese economy, commercial banks have been moving in step. After authorities in 2017 announced they would strengthen regulation to reduce risk for domestic firms investing abroad and curb irrational Belt and Road investment, China's largest state-owned commercial banks started to raise billions to fund investment under the Belt and Road. Industrial and Commercial Bank of China, the largest bank in the world by assets, is already taking part in 212 projects related to the Belt and Road, with credit facilities exceeding $67 billion. The first official Belt and Road bond in China's domestic market introduced a new financing instrument for the initiative. Hongshi Holding Group, a privately-owned cement-maker, issued a $47 million three-year corporate bond on the Shanghai Stock Exchange on January 19, 2018 Proceeds are earmarked for the purchase of equipment for a $300 million yuan cement plant in Laos with an expected daily capacity of 5,000 tons.

The Vision and Actions document describes the government's central role as marshaling domestic resources to provide stronger policy support for the Belt and Road. It will facilitate the establishment of the appropriate financial institutions and dedicated funds, while developing the right financial regulation to promote the initiative. Speaking at the China Development Forum in March 2018, Wang Zhaoxing, vice-chair of the newly formed China Banking and Insurance Regulatory Commission, said that its creation would provide a surer foundation for the financing of Belt and Road projects. "Banking and insurance integration is of benefit to strengthening regulation and expediting the healthy development of the banking and insurance sectors. At the same time, this is of benefit to fully using the rational integration of bank and insurance credit, bank loan capital and insurance capital sources to provide short and medium-term financing to One Belt One Road, and even infrastructure development."

The state remains firmly in charge of the financial system, being able to redirect immense financial resources to pursue its policy objectives when that is deemed useful or necessary. Although the largest commercial banks are prompted to compete against each other, they remain under state control. By operating as the state's bailout fund for the financial system, Central Huijin—a subsidiary of China's sovereign wealth fund—has become the largest shareholder in the main commercial banks. As a result, it holds the reins of the vital credit channels linking the financial system to the booming—and nominally independent—private sector.

Wang Yingyao shows that since the mid-1990s the Chinese state has "refashioned itself as a shareholder and institutional investor in the economy and resorted to financial means to manage its ownership, assets and public investments."[6] The state-owned banking system remains a critical instrument for managing development strategy, allocating credit to priority industries and projects, but the Chinese authorities know that they run the risk of exercising too much control over investment decisions at the expense of a more decentralized system for processing information, and one more clearly determined by a purely economic calculus. The risk of waste resulting from politically determined support for inefficient or unviable projects—"white elephants"—is a serious one. Even more damaging is the impact for the financial sector, which may be saddled with nonperforming loans, high leverage and unsustainable ratios. The Belt and Road may play an important role here, giving a general direction to economic development but leaving specific projects to be decided later and at the appropriate level—and preserving an element of competition between economic agents.

As in Taoist dialectics, the single concept first divides in two—land and sea—then in several—the corridors and countries—then in many—the specific projects and privileged locations. Taoism understands Tao as the one which connects the many. As the one divides in two, an alternating rhythm begins to pulsate between the poles, bringing the first wave motion into being.

The Belt

On land, there are three routes, understood as broad geographical areas. One from Northwest China and Northeast China to Europe and the Baltic Sea via Central Asia and Russia; one from Northwest China to the Persian Gulf and the Mediterranean Sea, passing through Central Asia and West Asia; and one from Southwest China through the Indochina Peninsula to the Indian Ocean. These three routes divide into six economic corridors con-

Belt geography

nected by six means of communication: "China has proposed a framework including six corridors, six means of communication, multiple countries, and multiple ports."[7] The Belt and Road will focus on jointly building a new Eurasian Land Bridge corridor and developing the China-Mongolia-Russia, China-Central Asia-West Asia and China-Indochina economic corridors by taking advantage of international transport routes, relying on core cities along the Belt and Road and using key economic industrial parks as cooperation platforms. The Vision and Actions document still described the China-Pakistan Economic Corridor and the Bangladesh-China-India-Myanmar Economic Corridor as "closely related to the Belt and Road Initiative," but since then they have been fully absorbed under the umbrella concept.

The China-Indochina corridor generally outperforms the others: China is an important destination of exports for all the countries, ranging from 5% of total Cambodian exports to 25.7% of total Laotian exports in 2015. The China-West Asia corridor is the weakest among the six, with the many countries along this corridor belonging to different economic groupings with limited institutional trade links to China.

The transport network, consisting of railways, highways, sea routes and air routes, together with the electric power transmission and telecommunication networks, and oil and gas pipelines, creates the connectivity network providing the physical infrastructure for the six economic corridors. When Chinese decision-makers argue that the Belt and Road is designed according to a sound understanding of the theory of economic development, what they have in mind is before all else the concept of an economic corridor.

Eco. corridor

Economic corridors are not transport connections along which people and goods move, but much more complex economic geographies taking advantage of both specialization and connectivity to bring about superior economic outcomes. While the traditional connectivity concept focuses on the end-points of the connection with limited consideration to what goes on between them, the economic corridor concept deliberately considers the whole space. This, incidentally, is why the initiative speaks of a "belt" rather than a "road" as its land component. On sea, only the end points are connected and thus the term "road" is appropriate there, but on land what is being envisioned is the fragmentation of production processes across different geographies. Unlike the original Silk Road, the Belt and Road is not predominantly about transportation infrastructure but about economic integration. The initiative does not attempt to unbundle production and consumption—the vision of the original Silk Road—but rather to unbundle different segments of the production chain, to build an expanded "factory floor" along the full economic corridor and across national borders.

Transport corridors usually transform into economic corridors though gradual development, urban agglomeration and division of labor leading to the formation of economic clusters. As Hasaan Khawar puts it, the Grand Trunk Road—the road running from Bangladesh to Afghanistan through Northern India and Pakistan—is a good example of this. The route has been in existence for more than two millennia, but only recently has it developed into a vibrant economic corridor. The idea behind the Belt and Road is to create economic corridors by design rather than letting them evolve naturally and slowly on their own. The level of investment being discussed cannot in any case be recouped through toll payments alone. It requires a much broader flow of future revenue. "Economic corridor development is therefore the only way to go."[8]

China has shown great interest in the construction of high-speed railways outside its borders, a technology that embodies its fast rise to technological preeminence. Freight rail links have been built, renovated or expanded in Uzbekistan, Kyrgyzstan,

Pakistan, Kazakhstan and elsewhere. China has long suggested constructing a railway connecting Kashgar in Xinjiang to the Fergana valley—the core of Central Asia—through Osh in Kyrgyzstan, a project that could permanently change centuries-old divisions around these mountains and plateaus. Perhaps even more visibly, new and efficient roads are being built all across the region. One of the most ambitious projects is the expansion of the Karakoram Highway linking Xinjiang to central Pakistan. Traveling along this route, I witnessed first-hand how colossal feats of engineering are opening up some of the most difficult terrains in the world to regular and fast traffic. In Pakistan the highway is being upgraded from Raikot to Thakot in Khyber Pakhtunkhwa province using a combination of grants and a concessional loan from Beijing totaling $150 million. A road realignment project is under way from Thakot to Havelian in Khyber Pakhtunkhwa using a $1.3 billion concessional loan. It involves the construction of seven tunnels and sixty-eight large bridges, and will be completed in 2020. All these construction projects have boosted the development and production of new machinery fit for purpose, such as the gigantic SLJ900/32, an all-in-one machine capable of carrying, lifting and placing sections of track, connecting pillar with pillar in suspended bridges, or the TBM Slurry for digging tunnels: weighing 4,000 tonnes, it has 100m of trailing infrastructure that enables workers to install the tunnel walls as the cutting head inches forward powered by hydraulic rams.

On the southern land route, China plans to connect Southeast Asian countries with the southwest region of Yunnan through a series of high-speed railways. There are three routes planned: a central one that runs through Laos, Thailand and Malaysia to reach Singapore; a western route through Myanmar; and an eastern one through Vietnam and Cambodia. Projects are at various stages of development, with construction in the Thailand and Laos legs already progressing.

The formal implementation of the United Nations TIR Convention in China is a milestone for the Belt and Road, which was always predicated on facilitating transit and customs procedures. The TIR system, based on the United Nations TIR Convention, serves as a global customs-clearance facilitator for international cross-border road transportation of goods. The only global customs transit system for moving goods across international borders, it has been supporting trade and development for more than sixty years, by allowing customs-sealed vehicles and freight containers to transit countries with minimal border checks. At present, there are seventy-three Contracting Parties to the TIR Convention, most of which are located along the Silk Road Economic Belt. China acceded to this Convention on July 5, 2016 as the 70th Contracting Party and the Convention entered into force for China on January 5, 2017. Currently, its pilot TIR gateways include Horgos in Xinjiang (bordering Kazakhstan), Irkeshtam in Xinjiang (bordering Kyrgyzstan), Erenhot in Inner Mongolia (bordering Mongolia), Manzhouli in Inner Mongolia (bordering Russia), Suifenhe Port in Heilongjiang (also bordering Russia) and Dalian in Liaoning (the trade gateway towards the Pacific).

Industrial parks and free-trade zones play an important role in the planning and development of economic corridors. China is quickly developing a number of overseas industrial development zones with sound infrastructure, clear industrial focus and access to a full range of public services. These zones give rise to a geographic network of highly concentrated but interconnected businesses.

By 2016 a progress report on the Belt and Road already enumerated eighteen border cooperation zones and fifty-two industrial parks as being operational across eighteen countries.[9] A particularly notable case is the Horgos International Cooperation Center, which I visited in June 2016. This is a free trade and free movement zone built across the border between China and Kazakhstan. Goods sold inside the Cooperation Center may be carried across the border free of tariffs. People too may circulate inside the area without having to transit a border post. The border between the two countries has in fact been rendered just as invisible as, say, that between Belgium and the Netherlands.

In July 2018 a new financial hub opened in Astana, the Kazakh capital, explicitly presented as part of the critical financial infrastructure for the Belt and Road. Both the Shanghai Stock Exchange and the state-run Silk Road Fund became shareholders of the projects securities exchange, the Astana International Exchange. The Shanghai Stock Exchange is a 25 per cent shareholder. While contributing staff and resources, they are also providing a gateway to Chinese funds and Chinese brokers. More generally, the Astana International Financial Center hopes to attract players ranging from Chinese state funds to Swiss private banks by offering tax breaks, easy entry and a Common Law court. Capitalizing on its location at the intersection of different economic and political influences, it wants to serve as an arbitration center for contracts between Chinese and Russian companies, while employing its own court and arbitration center staffed with British judges and barristers.[10]

Kazakhstan is one of just two countries where the Belt is already having a visible and significant impact. Sharing a long border with Xinjiang province, benefitting from high levels of political stability and already enjoying some measure of economic development, it was always going to offer a privileged testing ground for the initiative. China sees Kazakhstan as its gateway to Europe and has encouraged the speedy development of some of the most emblematic local projects of the Belt and Road there. Even in the much more diffuse world of cultural exchange—the fifth pillar of the initiative—Kazakhstan is making strides. When in May 2018 China televised a live concert to celebrate the Belt and Road, only one foreigner performed: a singer, the announcer said, "with a clear voice and friendly eyes from Kazakhstan named Dimash." The *People's Daily* often mentions Dimash Kudaibergen in editorials on China's foreign policy, a symbol of cultural exchange and the new Chinese ability to attract talent from abroad.

Just across the border from Horgos, a major new dry port is being developed with the explicit ambition of organizing the network of future roads and railways connecting the Eurasian supercontinent. China and the European Union are already the two largest economies in the world, alongside the United States, and trade between them can be expected to keep growing and diversifying. Suppose you build a port right at the midway point between the two, where freight trains can converge, unload their containers and from which new trains, recombined according to their destination, will quickly depart. This would be just the start, though. Once the port is fully operational, one may expect new industrial areas and new cities to start emerging along the trade routes, taking advantage of the new infrastructure, low labour costs and growing industrial specialization in different economic regions. Chinese manufacturers in particular would certainly be attracted by the possibility of entering the Russia market without paying any duties. If they set up on the other side of the border, they can benefit from the fact that Russia and Kazakhstan—together with a number of smaller countries—are members of the Eurasian Economic Union, a customs union.

In May 2015 Presidents Putin and Xi signed a joint statement on integrating the Russia-led Eurasian Economic Union with the Belt and Road. From the start there had been fears that China's bold plans would necessarily clash with Russian interests. Beijing was well aware of the risk and in this case played its cards shrewdly. Many of the countries central to the Belt and Road were part of the traditional Russian sphere of influence in Central Asia—absorbed by the Soviet Union until 1991, of course—so

Russian opposition had the potential to place an impassable roadblock in China's way. Russia's decision to endorse the Belt and Road changed the parameters of the project. It gave the green light to China's ambitions for countries such as Kazakhstan and Georgia—its gateways to Europe—while focusing on trade integration as the next stage in the initiative. After all, the Eurasian Economic Union is a trade agreement, so any significant integration between the two structures promised concrete progress in the area of trade, potentially leading to new trade agreements in the future between China and the economic bloc led by Moscow, extending all the way to the Polish border.

It is undeniable that the Eurasian Economic Union and the Belt and Road are very different creatures. The former is overtly political and geopolitical, inward-oriented and committed to developing a common institutional framework. Its model is the European Union. As a result, it is focused on very detailed economic and technical cooperation and integration in every economic sector, aiming for a high level of coherence and harmonization. The Belt and Road is a more original idea. It is less rigid, less committed to legal and institutional forms, more ambitious in its geographic scope and economic impact, while remaining focused on concrete projects to be developed across borders. Its focus on investment and infrastructure follows naturally.[11] It is not clear, however, that these differences in nature are an obstacle to increased cooperation between the two initiatives. Difference can be interpreted as complementarity.

In May 2018 China and the Eurasian Economic Union signed a free-trade agreement in Astana. While non-preferential—meaning tariffs are not cancelled—the agreement will make it possible to improve conditions for access of goods to the market through norms for trade facilitation and improve the level of interaction across all spheres of trade cooperation. The first major systematic arrangement ever reached between the two sides, it covers thirteen chapters, including customs cooperation, trade facilitation, intellectual property rights, sectoral cooperation and government procurement, as well as e-commerce and competition. In an interview with Xinhua, Tigran Sargsyan, the chairman of the board to the Eurasian Economic Commission, said that the treaty "creates a serious legal framework for the interaction of businesses and makes the environment in which they will operate predictable." *+ w/ China*

The other country where the Belt and Road is already having a significant impact—and one central to its success—is Pakistan. If Kazakhstan serves as China's gateway to Europe, Pakistan is its gateway to the Indian Ocean. Because the strategic alliance between the two countries goes back decades, it was expected that swift progress could be expected in developing an economic corridor starting from Kashgar in Xinjiang and reaching Karachi and Gwadar. As Andrew Small argues, the close security and political relationship between the two sides means that Pakistan has a unique level of comfort with the strategic elements of the initiative, including, for instance, ports that can serve both commercial and military purposes.[12]

The success of the project did not in this case depend on third countries, so it offered a more manageable scale than the larger Belt and Road, where it must sometimes seem that too many variables are simultaneously in play. In this case the forces bringing the two economies closer together do not need to be conjured up by the Belt and Road. They were already powerful before the initiative, which is therefore—in this case at least—required primarily to organize rather than to create, an easier task. No less important, Pakistan is rich in natural resources and has a vast internal market, two points of great interest to China. Its planning authorities are looking for large markets, with significant growth potential, capable of matching China's own scale of development. With 200 million inhabitants, Pakistan is a valuable asset for the Belt and Road. Or, as Wang Yi, China's foreign minister, prefers to put it, "if One Belt One Road is like a symphony involving and benefiting every country, then construction of the China-Pakistan Economic Corridor is the sweet melody of the symphony's first movement."

The 2017 Pakistani film *Chalay Thay Saath* (They Went Together) portrays how a Chinese backpacker and a Pakistani doctor, thrown together during a group-tour road trip, improbably but inevitably fall in love. Director Umer Adil explained that his inspiration for the script came from the decades-long relationship between China and Pakistan, represented by the Karakoram Highway, built seventy years ago. As the couple must deal with various roadblocks—language barriers, racist stereotypes, familial disapproval, and even a deadly flood that, for a time, erects a physical barrier between them—their story offered a popular image or symbol for the China-Pakistan Economic Corridor and the difficulties involved in realizing it.[13]

The China-Pakistan Economic Corridor is a development corridor covering Xinjiang province and the entire territory of Pakistan. Its spatial layout is described as comprising one belt, three axes and several passages. The belt refers to the organizing central structure, including Kashgar, Tumshuq city, and Atushi city and Akto county in Kizilsu Kirghiz autonomous prefecture of Xinjiang, China, as well as Islamabad, parts of Punjab, Sindh, Khyber-Pakhtunkhwa, Balochistan, AJK and Gilgit in Pakistan. The three axes refer to three horizontal axes intersecting the belt. The passages refer to several railways and highway trunk lines from Islamabad to Karachi and Gwadar.

The orderly flow of economic factors in both countries "will significantly improve the resource allocation efficiency and bring into full play the comparative advantage of each country."[14] China and Pakistan are expected to strengthen cooperation in trade and industrial areas, expand bilateral economic and trade relations, and enhance the level of bilateral trade liberalization. They should cooperate in key areas, enhance the effectiveness of cooperation and strive to achieve synchronization, coordination and reciprocity of economic development. Specific sectors to be actively promoted include textiles, the production of parts and components for industry, and agriculture. There is a plan to extract coal in the Thar desert at one of the world's biggest known deposits of lignite, a lower-grade brown version of the fuel. The project includes the building of power plants to expand capacity in a country that faces chronic electricity shortages. The first phase, which will add 660 megawatts of power, will be completed in 2019 and can be scaled to 5,000 megawatts to make it the largest cluster of electricity production in Pakistan.[15] In all these projects, the two countries should "give full play to their own comparative advantages."

A central priority is the construction and development of Gwadar city and port. The project has acquired a highly symbolic status for the Belt and Road as a whole. On the one hand, Gwadar lies in a privileged strategic position, with a claim to becoming a new Chinese coastal city—in economic terms at least it will play that role, linking the western provinces of China to the Indian Ocean. The vision for the city is suitably ambitious: the port will be combined with a new expressway, international airport, an industrial park, and even world-class tourism facilities. The industrial park provides foreign investors with 100 per cent ownership, a twenty-three-year tax holiday, and an exemption on custom duties for material used in the construction and operation of the port. Today more than 1,000 people already work at the 660-meter container terminal. A leading Chinese investment company announced it will invest $500 million in the first phase of a project aimed at building homes for around 500,000 incoming Chinese professionals expected in Gwadar by 2023. "China Pak Hills will be the first development of its kind in Gwadar.

A mixed-use gated development tailor-made for Chinese professionals in Gwadar, it will offer an all-encompassing lifestyle to live, work and play, with a host of facilities that will set the benchmark of future developments. The company building the model city has an annual turnover of around $10 billion. The aim of this project is to build infrastructure for the incoming influx of Pakistani and Chinese professionals. Growth in Gwadar will go up massively and it will need strong social infrastructure to cater for this need."[16]

A quiet fishing village may soon become a major cosmopolis, a new Dubai. What better image could one find of the transformative power of the Belt and Road?

The Road

The Vision and Actions document proposed two routes for the Maritime Silk Road. The East Route would start from China's coast through the South China Sea to the South Pacific. The West Route would pass through the South China Sea and terminate in Africa and Europe. This scheme was slightly modified in a 2017 document entitled Vision for Maritime Cooperation under the Belt and Road Initiative, where three separate routes are envisioned. First, the China-Indian Ocean-Africa-Mediterranean Sea Blue Economic Passage linking the China-Indochina Peninsula Economic Corridor, running westward from the South China Sea to the Indian Ocean, and connecting the China-Pakistan Economic Corridor (CPEC) and the Bangladesh-China-India-Myanmar Economic Corridor (BCIM-EC). Second, the "blue economic passage" of China-Oceania-South Pacific, traveling southward from the South China Sea into the Pacific Ocean. Another passage is also envisioned leading up to Europe via the Arctic Ocean. With perfect symmetry, both the Silk Road Economic Belt and the Maritime Silk Road now encompass three routes each.

NUTS AND BOLTS

The initiative will focus on jointly building smooth, secure and efficient transport routes connecting major sea ports along the Eurasian littoral. A number of opportunities for cooperation along the route have been identified, including maritime transport and infrastructure, resource development, marine scientific research, joint law enforcement, and maritime security. Exchanges and coordination with relevant countries are encouraged. Closer cooperation will be carried out to improve the market environment for international transportation and to facilitate maritime transportation. China is willing to enhance customs cooperation with countries along the Road, and to promote information exchange, mutual recognition of customs regulations, and mutual assistance in law enforcement. Chinese enterprises will be encouraged to participate in the construction and operation of overseas ports, something already well under way. According to research conducted by the *Financial Times*, nearly two-thirds of the world's top sixty container ports had received some degree of Chinese investment by 2015. During the first half of 2017, Chinese companies unveiled plans to buy or invest in nine overseas ports, five of which are in the Indian Ocean. Four separate initiatives are set for Malaysia, with Chinese company investments scheduled for the $7.2 billion Melaka Gateway, the $2.84 billion Kuala Linggi Port, the $1.4 billion Penang Port and the $177 million Kuantan port projects, according to company announcements.

Since the turn of the century Chinese companies have been involved in the construction, management and expansion of numerous port facilities, from Hambantota in Sri Lanka to Gwadar in Pakistan, Kyaukpyu in Myanmar and Doraleh in Djibouti. A principal category covers hub ports, servicing huge container ships and transshipping them onto smaller vessels to connect with regional ports. A second category, as David Brewster describes it, should not be overlooked and is perhaps more significant: ports such as Gwadar and Kyaukpyu are meant to connect the Indian Ocean with China via overland transport corridors.[17] Pakistan and Myanmar may become China's California, granting it access to a second ocean and resolving the Malacca dilemma. Access to the offshore gas fields in the Bay of Bengal was always central to the Kyaukpyu project. The gas pipeline will carry up to 12 billion cubic meters of gas annually. The oil pipeline—running in parallel and with a capacity of 22 million barrels of oil per year, about 6 per cent of China's 2016 oil imports—was built to transport oil from the Middle East and Africa directly to China, avoiding the Malacca Strait and cutting shipping distances by 1200 km. Even more dramatically, using overland pipelines connected to Gwadar will reduce the distance from the Persian Gulf to just 2,500 km—but the pipeline will depend on ultra high-power pumping stations as it has to pass through the Karakoram Pass, at an altitude of 5,000 to 6,000 meters above Gwadar or Kashgar. On existing routes via the Malacca Strait, oil tankers need to travel more than 10,000 km for two to three months to reach China. While ports such as Hambantota are close to existing shipping lines, others such as Gwadar presuppose a significant redrawing of those lines in the future.

Another central driver of the Road concerns the growing trade links between China and India. Given their size and proximity, the two countries are bound to develop the world's largest trading relationship. In turn this will have to be based on gigantic infrastructure projects along the Indian Ocean coast or by train through Myanmar and Bangladesh. It was not surprising, therefore, to find that the port of Kolkata featured prominently in the original plans for the Road, with the Indian city appearing on the famous map of the initiative published by Xinhua. The port could be an important conduit in developing value chains connecting Chinese and Indian manufacturers, but more recently it has been dropped from all official references, as India increasingly distanced itself from the Belt and Road. Much of the success of the initiative depends on whether this can be corrected in the future.

Other inefficiencies may in time be eliminated. By enhancing port infrastructure in the Mediterranean, it should be feasible to transport cargo from China and Asia via shorter shipping lines. Antwerp, Hamburg, London, and Rotterdam are the main ports where containers are discharged today and the cargo distributed all over Europe. With its engagement in Mediterranean ports like Piraeus and potentially Trieste, Venice or Istanbul, China may hope to start changing the spatial pattern of the container shipping system. For decades, we have been discussing a possible shift of the traditional dominance of Northern European ports to Southern Europe. The Road may make it a reality.

Bypassing the Malacca strait by building a canal through the Kra Isthmus in Thailand—around 100 km long and 25 meters deep, it would take ten years to build—could be an even greater game changer. From a shipping perspective, it would mean shorter and cheaper—perhaps two or three days faster—shipping lanes for all, but a number of countries, including the United States, may resist the idea because it would also mean the speedier deployment of the Chinese navy to the Indian Ocean. It is unclear why Thailand should welcome a project that would give physical and symbolic meaning to the country's division and embolden the Muslim insurgency raging in the south. The canal would necessarily be wider than the Chao Phraya River, the nation's main north-south waterway that travels through Bangkok and by the royal Grand Palace, viewed by many as the vital ligament holding Thailand together. Political geography in the whole region would be radically redesigned, but the Chinese ambassador to Thailand has privately asserted that the Kra Canal is part of China's vision for the Belt and Road and a Chinese construction company involved in recent land reclamation and island-building in the South China Sea has expressed interest in the project.[18]

Finally, there is the Arctic. In January 2018 the State Council Information Office published a white paper titled "China's Arctic Policy," whose main premise is that global warming will turn the Arctic into a new area for economic activity and state competition. The opening sentences in the paper are unusually frank: "Global warming in recent years has accelerated the melting of ice and snow in the Arctic region. As economic globalization and regional integration further develops and deepens, the Arctic is gaining global significance for its rising strategic, economic values and those relating to scientific research, environmental protection, sea passages, and natural resources." As the ice melts, conditions for the development of the Arctic may be gradually changed, offering opportunities for the commercial use of sea routes and development of resources in the region. Predictions indicate that the Bering Strait will open for an extended period around 2020, the Northern Sea Route around 2025, and the Transpolar Route around 2030. The Northwest Passage will open last.[19] Responding to these opportunities, China hopes to build a "Polar Silk Road" along the Arctic shipping lanes, the third main sea route of the Belt and Road. Shipping through the Northern Sea Route would shave almost twenty days off the regular passage time using the traditional route through the Suez Canal. Another section of the paper focuses on how China can use the Arctic's resources, including fossil fuels and fisheries. Among China's main interests in the region is its major stake in Russia's Yamal liquefied natural gas project which is expected to supply China with four million tonnes of LNG per annum.

* * *

Just as with the land component, infrastructure development along the Maritime Silk Road is no more than the beginning of the story. The initiative does not stop at creating a dense network of ports along the Indian Ocean. It is also and perhaps primarily about boosting growth and industrialization across the region through heavy investment in infrastructure—the creation of "strategic propellers for hinterland development," as the Vision and Actions document calls it. The mistake is to think that the new sea lines of communication are meant to connect existing poles of economic activity. China takes a much more integrated or comprehensive approach to economic development. As the name of the project indicates, the Maritime Silk Road is meant to build a new economic landscape for the twenty-first century, often considering transport as but one leg of a much broader development and industrialization project, what Chinese media and official documents call the "Ports-Park-City" model of development. When a state-run Chinese company, the Guangxi Beibu Gulf International Port Group, announced its intention to expand the capacity of the deep-water container port in Kuantan in Malaysia, the investment was to be combined with the construction of a new industrial park and steel plant.

When I went to Djibouti in December 2017 I saw how the Chinese approach involves a vast and complex network of communication arteries branching out into smaller passages. Salt deposits mined in Lake Assal were transported by truck—on a road financed by the European Union—to an expanding salt port in the Goubet from which small boats could carry it to the large Doraleh port. This had been recently constructed with Chinese capital and under Chinese management. I was shown the areas reserved for a future industrial zone and, next to the port, the first Chinese overseas military base, a dark and impenetrable fortress, hidden from prying eyes crossing the Tadjoura gulf by the walls of containers and giant cranes stationed in the port. A number of sources told the *Global Times* in July 2018 that the military base gives Chinese businessmen more confidence to invest in Djibouti. Whether that is because it will contribute to long-term stability in the country or because the local government will hesitate before taking decisions detrimental to Chinese interests was left unsaid.[20]

Like many of the projects along the Maritime Silk Road, Doraleh port is a slowly expanding project. Its initial rationale was to serve landlocked Ethiopia, a country of 100 million inhabitants where China wants to move some of its low-end manufacturing, such as footwear and apparel. For that purpose, it has financed and built a new fast railway linking Addis Ababa and Djibouti, one that—as I found out—is operated by Chinese staff. But the economic rationale for Doraleh goes far beyond East Africa. Djibouti is located on the main trade route linking Europe and Asia, so presumably it can become a trans-shipment hub, a process already under way. Some have even started to contemplate a railway linking Djibouti to Cameroon and Nigeria, transforming Doraleh into a serious rival to the Suez Canal.

In Djibouti I could not help but be struck by the profusion of competing major ports. Literally next door to the Chinese-built Doraleh I visited the container terminal operated by Dubai-based DP World, unanimously considered the most technologically advanced container terminal in Africa. Asking whether the two ports might not be somewhat redundant, I was assured they were not competing against each other, but the truth is that just two months after my visit the Djibouti government—pressured by China—seized control of the DP World port in Doraleh. China was exercising its political and economic power to sidestep rivals in a bid to consolidate control over all the major shipping lanes in the Indian Ocean. In December 2017 Sri Lanka formally handed over commercial activities in its main southern port to the same Chinese company managing Doraleh, but Djibouti raised more delicate questions. Would the large American base established in Djibouti have secure access to supplies if the two major ports in the country were controlled by China?

China Merchants, the company running both Doraleh and Hambantota in Sri Lanka, has a long history steeped in the structures of global capitalism. Founded in 1873, its primary purpose was to compete with foreign companies that operated steamships in Chinese waters. Its founder, Li Hongzhang, saw an opportunity to draw Chinese capital invested in foreign firms to a new company. By 1877 it owned thirty steamships and could boast the highest tonnage among steamship companies in China—just the achievement Deng Xiaoping would have envied at the beginning of his efforts to modernize China's merchant navy a hundred years later. Remarkably, having survived for almost 150 years through a number of radical transformations— in 1951 the Central Government reorganized the Shanghai Head Office of China Merchants into the People's Navigation Company and merged it with the General Navigation Office under the Ministry of Communications—China Merchants has emerged as a core company of the Belt and Road, whose main presuppositions are those held by Li Hongzhang in the nineteenth century: the global economy embodies deep structures of power and if China wants to occupy the center of the system and infuse it with its own ideas, it needs to think and act globally and compete with foreigners on the same scale. Even the initial success of the company seemed to anticipate the Chinese economic model of our time, being the result of the combination of the government's financial support and the merchant managers' autonomy.[21]

* * *

Maps of the Maritime Silk Road released by the Chinese media have shown the route running through disputed areas in the South China Sea, another hot spot for geopolitical rivalry. The contradiction is that the South China Sea is the geographic area where China has been developing a new, more assertive and confrontational foreign policy, and it lies at the very center of those free and safe shipping lanes evoked by every official document on the Belt and Road. There are two main ways to think about this contradiction. One could argue that the Road is meant to bring about new forms of cooperation and that these can in time replace the logic of competition now ruling disputes in the area. Alternatively, it is possible to conceive that China—shying away from open military conflict—regards the Road as a way to settle the issue by economic means and infrastructure development. Countries such as Malaysia, the Philippines and Vietnam continue to hesitate between adopting one of the two interpretations of the initiative.

In the past China has used economic aid as a powerful tool in advancing its interests in the South China Sea. When President Hu Jintao visited Phnom Penh in 2012 he promised his Cambodian counterpart economic assistance of 450 million yuan. A few months later Cambodia opposed including a mention of the South China Sea dispute in a joint statement tabled by Vietnam and the Philippines. Around the same time, Chinese quarantine authorities reportedly blocked hundreds of container lorries of Philippine bananas from entering Chinese ports. China accounted for more than 30 per cent of Philippine banana exports.

The Maritime Silk Road will advance Chinese interests in the South China Sea in different ways. First, it can further develop points of pressure and reward similar to those used with Cambodia and the Philippines in 2012. Second, cooperative projects may be relied upon to reduce tensions. Third, and equally important, strengthened institutional links are expected to foster the view that maritime affairs and disputes should be handled and resolved by directly concerned parties, avoiding the involvement of outside actors such as the United States.[22]

Countries in Southeast Asia are not oblivious to the geopolitical consequences of the economic project. The epochal dispute over land features and territorial waters in the South China Sea will shift in China's favor once shipping lanes in the region grow in significance and come to be dominated by Chinese companies, while the vast majority of ports will be controlled by China and could have dual civilian and military uses. China passed a law in 2016 creating a legal framework for the use of civilian assets to support military logistics operations and requiring all Chinese industries that conduct international transportation to provide supplies and aid to the Chinese navy as needed. In July 2018 a document issued by Hainan province, which administers the country's claimed islands and waters in the contested South China Sea, announced that "any entity or individual" who wishes to develop uninhabited islands can apply and provide development plans to provincial ocean administration authorities. According to the report, the timeframe for developing the uninhabited islands varies depending on use. For aquaculture, they can be used for fifteen years, tourism and amusement projects allow for twenty-five years, salt and mineral industry projects for thirty years, public welfare projects for forty years and harbor- and shipyard-building projects for fifty years. It said developers will have to pay the government for the use of the islands, which would also benefit Beijing's goal of building a free-trade zone for economic development.

For South China Sea littoral states, the specter of Chinese naval and coast-guard assets patrolling vital shipping sea lines and waters adjacent to these ports may actually dissuade them from participating in the scheme lest it be seen as jeopardizing their own territorial and maritime claims.[23] Every entanglement with the initiative, however, offers pressure points that China can use to promote new projects and closer relationships. *or constrain*

In 2014 an article in the Mandarin-language *Pacific Journal* *Ch.* spelled out the country's Indian Ocean strategy in the form of a sixteen-character guideline: "Select locations meticulously, make deployments discreetly, give priority to cooperative activities and penetrate gradually." This expansion must be done with caution, low-pitched and slow-paced, doing its utmost to maintain the relative balance of power in the Indian Ocean. The so-called "meticulous selection" refers to the current development of China's maritime power. It proceeds carefully by selecting several key ports to build overseas bases, the sinews of Chinese maritime power. China needs to build at least one military base in each of the key waters of the Indian Ocean. First, in the Bay of Bengal, China's maritime power needs to exert effective strategic influence on the western mouth of the Malacca Strait, and it must also implement reliable protection for the Sino-Myanmar oil and gas pipeline. Second, in the Arabian Sea and the Persian Gulf, China's maritime power has to ensure that the oil produced from the Persian Gulf is safely transported and the national energy supply guaranteed. Third, in the Western Indian Ocean, China's maritime powers need to respond to non-traditional security threats such as the Suez-Red Sea-Aden Gulf route and piracy on the east coast of Africa.

"Slow penetration" aims to reduce the suspicion of hostile maritime hegemony in India and the United States. "When constructing a point layout, try to construct as low as possible, develop as high-profile as possible in security cooperation, and do more meticulous work such as marine survey, marine surveying and mapping, port assistance, disaster relief, and try to extend the tentacles and build a good relationship. Embrace the ground, lay a solid foundation, accumulate strength, wait and use appropriate opportunities, take advantage of opportunities like the United Nations mandate to fight Somali pirates."[24]

THE BELT AND ROAD
AND THE WORLD ECONOMY

The main question to which the Belt and Road aims to offer an answer is that of China's position in the global economic system. For more than thirty years, China has moved along a fast trajectory of economic growth exhibiting a remarkably stable trend, but the inevitable consequence is that its economy has changed along the way. Many of the factors that made this economic miracle possible are no longer present, which means that more radical changes have become mandatory. The story of the past thirty years is unlikely to repeat itself, even if China remains a success story. Growth dynamics in the real world do not follow linear relations. To some extent they remain unpredictable. Many famous success stories have ended in rapid slowdowns and long periods of stagnation, appearing just at those times when everyone had stopped fearing them.

Until now the story in China has been one of supple adaptation. After Deng's liberal reforms, the Chinese economy was quickly integrated into the global economy, taking full advantage of newly developing value chains. The fact that these international value chains were increasingly fragmented meant that China could specialize in limited segments, where it had obvious advantages of scale or low-labor costs. In the past, many developing countries had struggled with the challenges of having to learn too much in too short a period, the only way to catch up with more advanced economies. To give one example, it was difficult to learn how to produce an automobile that could compete in the global market, while becoming a world leader in auto components can be done far more easily. Instead of having to make the whole car industry competitive, a developing nation can gain competitiveness in a single stage of production. Taking advantage of internationally fragmented value chains, China was able to approach the development process in a piecemeal fashion. "By allowing developing nations to focus on one part or one stage at a time, the global value chain revolution made knowledge absorption easier. The requisite technology and skills base for making a product could be digested bit by bit."[1]

The offshoring of production stages meant that rich-nation firms sent their marketing, managerial, and technical know-how along with the production stages that had been moved offshore. What Richard Baldwin calls the "second unbundling"—or the "global value chain revolution"—redrew the boundaries of competitiveness. Revolutionary advances in information and communication technology changed the cost-benefit analysis by making it much easier to coordinate different stages of production at great distances. Suddenly it became possible to move knowledge across continents almost as easily as it had been to move commodities and finished goods—and if knowledge was evenly available, why not put it to use where labor was cheaper? Many multinationals did just that and this high-tech low-wage combination quickly became the model for every major multinational. All the Chinese authorities needed to do was create the channels through which knowledge could flow unimpeded.

The serendipitous coincidence of so many favorable factors has only recently begun to erode. In late 2003 labour shortages first started to appear in southeastern coastal cities in China. To solve the problem, cities in Guangdong, southern China, were forced to increase the local minimum wage level. It was only the start of a self-feeding process which has predictably picked up speed, no doubt helped by the swift aging of the country's population. Between 2009 and 2013, Chinese wages surged 5.7 per cent, 19.3 per cent, 21.2 per cent, 11.8 per cent and 13.9 per cent, according to data from China's National Bureau of Statistics. The 2013 wages of Chinese migrant workers increased at nearly twice the growth rate of China's GDP.

Many who see China's huge labor force as a decisive advantage also worry that robots and artificial intelligence will eventually take away the majority of jobs. Intriguingly, if robots and artificial intelligence are to become the dominant drivers of production in the coming century, having too large a population to care for could turn out to be more of a hindrance than an advantage. Perhaps this consideration helps explain why the Chinese Communist Party is fixated on the social and economic impact of artificial intelligence.[2]

The disappearance of traditional sources of growth is not limited to abundant unskilled labour. Technology transfers from advanced economies and high returns on capital investment have started to peter out. Local governments' heavy reliance on fiscal policy periodically results in large property bubbles and massive investment in heavy industry and construction threatens environmental sustainability. All these signs seem to indicate that China is a prime candidate for what development economists call "a middle-income trap". The term captures a situation where a country can no longer compete internationally in standardized, labor-intensive commodities because wages are relatively too high, but neither can it compete in higher value added activities on a broad enough scale because productivity—constrained by structural factors—remains relatively too low.

In 2015 China's finance minister, Lou Jiwei, took the unusual step of publicly conceding that China had a 50 per cent chance of falling into the much-dreaded trap. Speaking at a conference at Tsinghua University, Lou argued that the government needed to solve the problem of structural imbalances and market distortions in the economy within the next five to seven years while maintaining 6.5 to 7 per cent growth in order to avoid the middle-income trap. To that end, he highlighted reforms in five sectors, including encouraging imports of agricultural products, accelerating reform of the *hukou* (household registration) system, speeding up human resources reform, pushing rural land reforms, as well as tackling social security system-related issues. Agriculture is a particularly important case. Lou argued that China needs to encourage more food imports so that it can transfer rural laborers to fill vacancies at industrial and services sectors. He called for a reduction in subsidies for farmers, urging the country to import more farm goods from abroad. "Many Chinese have this war mentality and believe the country's food security will be endangered if war breaks out." Encouraging more farm goods imports in a secure and reliable way is, as we shall see, one of the goals of the Belt and Road.

Middle-income economies typically struggle to replace the old growth drivers with productivity growth, which depends on the accumulation of human capital and innovation and has a much longer time scale. Fostering innovation on a broad scale is a complex process and requires time to diffuse knowledge across the production process and build the necessary institutional structures. In the absence of major reforms, China will get squeezed between low-wage competitors in mature industries, and rich-country innovators in industries with rapid technological change. As Wang Jisi puts it, "it is being obstructed from the front and pursued at the rear. At the front there are developed countries, which occupy the high end of the industry chain, possess advanced technology, and are pushing for the revival of their own manufacturing industries. To the rear there are the South East Asian, South Asian, and African countries, which are catching up by using their advantage in low cost manufacturing." The metaphor of the Middle Kingdom has acquired a new and ominous meaning.

How is China to catapult itself from the position of a middle-income country to the top of the pyramid? A number of difficulties immediately present themselves. In the past the Chinese economy has been moving into empty economic space, occupying the segments of production vacated by earlier developers. The task now—moving to the top—is structurally different since, in some dimensions at least, that space is already occupied. Can China find markets for its growing high-tech industry and services if global markets in those areas are dominated by American and European firms? Can it reliably invest in a new economic paradigm without access to those markets? And how can it expect to enter them if standards—key technologies—are owned by foreign firms who thus have access to steady flows of revenue from royalties and licensing fees? Finally, were China to move into higher-value production segments, who would take its place producing lower-value goods, which in many cases are actually indispensable components and inputs? Countries like South Korea and Singapore could rely on the massive Chinese manufacturing base for that, but what happens when China tries to replicate the same process?

I am highlighting these questions to show the ways in which the world economy must be perceived as an interdependent whole. A trajectory of economic growth is not incompatible with taking a lower position in the hierarchical ladder—being on the periphery of the system rather than the center—but contradictions between the needs of the system and those of some countries are bound to arise. In many cases, a country will be unable to change its economy in a particular direction without altering the way the world economy is organized. A policy of economic development—if it is to chart a sustainable course—must take the form of a global policy. The Belt and Road is China's global development policy.

This approach comes naturally to the Chinese authorities. The tradition of Tianxia is—as we saw in an earlier chapter—a way to think about the "world" rather than the individual state. It stresses the relations of interdependence between individual units in a system and takes that insight to its logical conclusion. It is reinforced by Marxist thought, perhaps the Western intellectual tradition that comes closest to Tianxia on this point. From Lenin's theory of imperialism to Wallerstein's world-systems theory, a range of Marxist writers have insisted that the unit of social reality within which we operate, whose rules constrain us, is for the most part the world economy. In Beijing, these writers have been and remain in vogue.

Chinese decision-makers share with their Western counterparts the premise that economic and financial globalization has made it difficult for a single country to pursue a specific economic vision. But the Chinese are much less inclined to renounce all forms of economic planning than to redefine the rules of the globalization game. A priority identified in the Vision and Actions document is to improve the "division of labor and distribution of industrial chains." When it comes to the division of labor along the value chains of industrial production, positions and preferences that reflect the national interests of countries in the regions of the Belt and Road may differ or even contradict each other. In such cases, observers should be under no illusions that China, as the promoter of the initiative, is uniquely placed to pursue its interests.

Patterns of international specialization and division of labor are particularly relevant in the age of global value chains. Today, very few products are manufactured in a single country. A country's manufacturing imports are more likely to be intermediate goods—that is, commodities, components, or semi-finished products that a country uses to make its own products. These could be final products or new segments in a global network of producers and suppliers. One third of China's imports are destined for export processing zones, which account for almost half of the country's exports. Global value chains can become so complex that imports can also contain returned value added that originated in the importing country. In China, nearly 7 per cent of the total value of imported intermediate goods reflects value added that originated in China. For electronic goods, Chinese intermediate imports contain over 12 per cent of returned Chinese domestic value added.[4]

With the emergence of global value chains, the mercantilist approach that views exports as good and imports as bad starts to look counterproductive and even self-contradictory. If a country imposes high tariffs and obstacles on the imports of intermediate goods, its exports will be the first to suffer. As a number of studies by the OECD have shown, nominal duties on gross exports are an incomplete measure of effective tariff barriers. We must strip out the value of imported intermediaries used in making exports. The effective burden for the exporter is better measured by tariffs on the domestic value added of exports, and these tariffs can be larger than duties on gross exports by several orders of magnitude.

Domestic firms therefore need reliable access to imports of world-class goods and service inputs to improve their productivity and ability to export. In this new age, it pays to think across national borders. The global economy has a Tianxia feel. When intermediate inputs tend to cross borders many times, even small tariffs and border bottlenecks have a cumulative effect, and protective measures against imports increase the costs of production and reduce a country's export competitiveness.

These are all good arguments for trade liberalization—and it should therefore not surprise us that China has started vocally to defend the removal of barriers to cross-border flows of goods and services—but consider what happens to a country's ability to organize production along the most efficient lines. If goods are produced entirely in one country, that country has full control over the whole process. Once goods are produced in several countries as the combined result of an intricate division of labor in each value chain, things become more difficult. What a country wants is to pick and choose the best segments in each value chain. Industrial policy increasingly targets tasks rather than industries, but for that, a government would have to gain access to the levers of industrial policy in other countries, to be able to organize production across the whole value chain.

A country has far more to gain by moving into higher-value segments in a supply chain than by increasing productivity in an already-occupied segment. In truth, however, it is less a question of somersaulting to the top of extant value chains than building new ones, allowing one to specialize in capital-intensive and technology-intensive activities. If a country wants to compete with the most advanced economies, it must do so by establishing new—more efficient and more dynamic—value chains. We no longer live in a world where German and Chinese products compete against each other. More often what happens is that German-led value chains—including many international production stages—will be competing against Chinese-led value chains. As Richard Baldwin puts it, the offshoring of production tasks shifts the effective geographic boundaries of competition. The units facing each other in the global market are no longer nations but value chains—and that changes everything.[5]

Thus when China develops a policy toward important commodity producers, it is less interested in securing access to commodity markets than in building highly efficient value chains where it can occupy the top segment. It knows that its competitive advantage results from this organizing role.

An example may help understand the strategy at play. Because it wants to be the world leader in the electric-car market, China has been moving to lock up the supply for cobalt, an essential material to produce the lithium-ion batteries used in laptops, smartphones and, of course, electric cars. About 54 per cent of the global cobalt supply comes from the Democratic Republic of Congo and Chinese imports of cobalt from Congo totaled $1.2 billion last year. The second largest importer was India but with a negligible $3.2 million. Expectations of fast growth in the electric car market have caused cobalt prices to explode. But China is not interested in producing batteries. It wants to control the electric vehicles market. Given its size in the future and the need for reliable access to cobalt supplies, it may soon be in a position to determine who gets to become the largest electric car producer in the world.[6] Who rules cobalt commands the battery market; who rules the battery market commands the electric car market; who rules the electric car market commands the world.

Maximizing the value that is added by a nation's productive resources now involves deploying some of the resources abroad in global value chains. If China seeks to focus on certain segments of a given value chain, it needs high levels of complementarity in other countries. These will develop only if the right transportation and communications infrastructures have been put in place and if those countries adopt the right economic policy decisions. One Chinese expert told me that the Belt and Road is the first example of "transnational" industrial policy. "Formerly, all industrial policy was national," he said. He has a point, as even the European Union, when it created an ambitious transnational framework of rules and institutions, tended to abandon industrial policy on the grounds that it could not be reproduced at a transnational level. This points to the clash between different integration models.

The image of the original Silk Road is particularly misleading in this context. Transportation and communications networks are no doubt a precondition for the development of global value chains. But the crucial element is the set of industrial policy decisions by which countries strive to move into new chains or segments in an already-occupied value chain. China wants its industrial policy to be sufficiently coordinated with those of countries that occupy other segments and chains. In return, it can offer cheap financing and its experience of an economic model that has proved very successful in boosting industrialization and urbanization on an unprecedentedly fast timescale.

In practice, Chinese industry may need reliable suppliers of parts or intermediate goods, or it may build assembly plants overseas to avoid import tariffs, while keeping the bulk of the production chain in China. It may try to create new opportunities to export raw materials or intermediate goods produced in China or, conversely, to secure raw materials for its own industry on a stable basis. Given how important services have become to the integrity of global value chains, increasing service exports will also be a strategic goal for the Belt and Road.

Chinese policymakers are aware that some heavy industry in China will have to move abroad, and they have started looking at Central Asia, with its lower production costs, as a possible destination. As governments and the private sector in the region invest in energy development, transportation infrastructure, and residential construction, the demand for steel products in Central Asia is expected to boom in coming years, but Chinese producers have to compete with Russian, Turkish, and Ukrainian steel enterprises that benefit from easier trade regimes. These competitors would lose that advantage if Chinese companies established steel production units in Central Asian countries, which are rich in mineral resources and have low labor costs. In the integrated framework of the Silk Road Economic Belt, new transportation infrastructure could both boost demand for steel and prepare the ground for China to import steel from Central Asia as it moves into higher-value products and value-chain segments: grain-oriented silicon steel (electrical steel), steel sheet for nuclear power stations and steel for high-speed rail bogie frames and train wheels.

Soon after the launch of the Belt and Road, Hebei Province announced plans to move capacity for 5.2 million tons of steel, 5 million tons of cement and 3 million units of glass abroad by 2018. The targets for 2023 are even more ambitious, with capacity for 20 million tons of steel, 30 million tons of cement and 10 million units of glass waiting to be relocated abroad. Many projects are already underway. State-owned companies will help set up a 600,000 ton steel project in Thailand. In 2017 Tsingshan Group Holdings, a state-backed steel producer based in Wenzhou on China's southeastern coast, opened a two-million-ton stainless-steel plant on the Indonesian island of Sulawesi that accounts for 4 per cent of the world's stainless-steel production. The mill was built using a $570 million loan from the China Development Bank. Interestingly, Tsingshan's Indonesian plant is now exporting 300,000 metric tons of semi-finished stainless-steel slabs to the United States through a Pittsburgh joint venture. Tsingshan is expanding its Indonesian plant, and Jiangsu Delong, a Chinese producer based in Jiangsu province, is building another plant nearby. In Europe, after China's giant Hesteel took control over a Serbian mill in June 2016, the plant outside the small city of Smederevo could export tariff-free into the EU and to the US markets with minimum tariffs—until, of course, the 2018 additional Trump tariffs against European producers took effect.[7]

The problem of overproduction thus has a number of possible solutions. First, current production may find new markets in

Belt and Road countries. This will boost steel prices, helping Chinese companies and stabilizing the steel sector. Second, unused production capacity may find new outlets. Third, some of China's production capacity may actually be moved abroad. Gaining access to new cheap-labor pools and more favorable trade regimes, it can be placed on a sustainable path, guaranteeing cheap imports for Chinese industry, while simultaneously addressing some of China's environmental challenges. And to the extent that Chinese companies increasingly build plants overseas, these plants will become prime customers for machinery produced in the motherland.

* * *

"Digitalization has brought the Chinese people the historic opportunity of a millennium," wrote the Chinese researcher Zhi Zhenfeng in a commentary on Xi Jinping's speech to the National Cybersecurity Work Conference. "During the extended period of agrarian society, China was an economic power in the world, creating a resplendent culture, but it later missed out on the industrial revolution, missed an historic opportunity to progress along with the world, and it gradually slipped to a position where it was passively subjected to abuse."[8]

If the Belt and Road is to be understood as a form of transnational industrial policy, then China's own industrial strategy cannot be considered independently. While occupying the center of the initiative, the task of upgrading and accelerating technological development would be impossible without a full network of international industrial relations—as China's recent manufacturing strategy, Made in China 2025, puts it, a "new wave" of "industrial revolution" is tantamount to "reshaping the structure of the international division of labor." China will be able to focus on new technologies only to the extent that it can develop the highly elaborate global value chains upon which technological innovation depends. The strategy, approved in July 2015, unabashedly claims: "We will strive to transform China into the global manufacturing leader before the centennial of the founding of New China, which will lay the foundation for the realization of the Chinese dream to rejuvenate the Chinese nation." *Prob* The present moment, however, is fraught with danger. China finds itself on the cusp of falling into a middle-income trap. After the global financial crisis, developed countries have been attempting to revive their industrial sectors, as a response to both electoral discontent about job losses and the sense that manufacturing is entering a significant new revolution. Meanwhile, devel- oping countries are seeking to expand their share of global industrial labor and are investing in industrial capital to develop their export markets. Manufacturing in China is under enormous pressure from this "two-way squeeze" between developed and developing countries. The current model cannot address this challenge. Only a significant expansion in the technological content of Chinese manufacturing will do: "With resource and environmental constraints growing, costs of labor and production inputs rising, and investment and export growth slowing, a resource and investment intensive development model that is driven by expansion cannot be sustained. We must immediately adjust the development structure and raise the quality of development." The strategic task of transforming Chinese manufacturing "from large to strong" will be realized with the transformation from Made in China to Created in China, from China Speed to China Quality, and from Chinese Products to Chinese Brands.[9] In comparison to previous plans, Made in China 2025 expands its focus to capturing global market share, not just dominance in the China market, and is part of a broader strategy to use state resources to alter and create comparative advantage in strategic advanced technology industries on a global scale.

International industrial capacity cooperation under the Belt and Road encompasses arrangements by which Chinese companies can obtain technology from foreign entities. In May 2015, the State Council issued the Guiding Opinion on Promoting International Industrial Capacity and Equipment Manufacturing Cooperation, which identifies eleven sectors as priorities for international expansion: (1) steel and nonferrous metals, (2) construction materials, (3) rail equipment, (4) power generation and infrastructure, (5) resource development, (6) textiles, (7) automotive, (8) information technology, (9) machinery, (10) aviation, and (11) shipbuilding. Many of these sectors include activities Chinese industry wants to move abroad; in other cases, such as information and communications technology, the opinion calls for "promoting innovation upgrading" and "raising international competitiveness." To do this, authorities are directed to "encourage telecoms operating enterprises and Internet enterprises to use methods, including mergers and acquisitions and investments in infrastructure and facilities operations, to 'Go Out'."[10]

As early as 2006 the Overseas Investment Industrial Guiding Policy had identified certain categories of "encouraged-type overseas investment projects;" (1) investments that enable the acquisition of resources and raw materials that are in short supply domestically and which are "in urgent demand for national economic and social development;" (2) investments that support the export of products, equipment, technology, and labor for which China has a comparative advantage; and, (3) investments that "are able to clearly enhance China's technology research and development capacity, including an ability to use international leading technology and advanced management experience and professional talent." A recent State Council opinion clarifies and supplements this approach. In its Guiding Opinion on Further Guiding and Standardizing the Direction of Overseas Investment, issued in August 2017, the State Council reaffirmed the importance of "catalyzing the 'Going Out' strategy for products, technologies, and services." It also aims to expand the speed, scale, and efficacy of China's outbound investment, so as to promote the "transformation and upgrading of the domestic economy" and "international industrial capacity cooperation." In addition, the 2017 Investment Opinion redefines the broad categories of "encouraged" investments. Technology acquisition and utilization is a key consideration in determining whether a sector is "encouraged." For instance, the opinion encourages investments that strengthen "investment cooperation" with "overseas high and new technology and advanced manufacturing industry enterprises," as well as investments that promote the "sending out" from China to the world of "advantageous manufacturing capacity, advantageous equipment, and technology standards."[11] The Made in China 2025 strategy calls for "supporting enterprises to make acquisitions, equity investments, and venture investments overseas, and to establish R&D centers and testing bases and global distribution and services networks overseas."

In the past China has often tried to encourage technology transfers from Western multinationals. The difference now is that Made in China 2025 aims to develop the major industries of the future and the technologies being procured in Europe and the United States are less the finished product than the critical knowledge base for indigenous technological revolutions. Worldwide acquisitions by Chinese companies now resemble acquisitions by leading Western companies. They are not safe capital investments but ways to accelerate internal innovation processes and move into fast-growing business areas.

That transformation—so abundantly proclaimed in official Chinese documents—convinced Western governments and companies that the current wave of technology transfers may well be the last, drying up the source of Chinese high-value imports, investment and licensing fees. It is hardly surprising, then, that the strategy led to increasingly negative responses from Berlin, Brussels and other capitals. A strongly worded report from the

European Union Chamber of Commerce in China argued that China's top-down approach to drive industrial development would hurt the Chinese economy, while pointing out that "it would likely lead to the same tensions that have plagued China's trade relations with Europe and others over overcapacity in sectors like steel and aluminum."[12]

In Germany the general view of China has been steadily changing, as many in the German industry realize that the times when the two economies benefited from perfect complementarity are almost certainly behind us. The strategic industries where China wants to become the dominant global player are just those that Germany chose for its own industrial plans: robotics, automated vehicles, aerospace, artificial intelligence. Whereas one or two decades ago Germany could export its machinery to China sure in the knowledge that no Chinese firm could make the same sophisticated machines—and these were the machines China needed for its industrial and infrastructure boom—now Chinese competitors are present in the same sectors, a shift that was accelerated by European suppliers selling co-designed parts to the Chinese. In early August 2018 the German government decided to ban for the first time the sale of a German company to a Chinese suitor—a watershed moment. The decision to block the sale of machine tool company Leifeld Metal Spinning AG to a Chinese company came after an extensive review that led the government to conclude that such a transaction would be a risk to "public order and safety". Chancellor Merkel's government wants to keep the company's expertise in the field of rocket and nuclear technology out of Chinese hands. It remained unclear whether national security arguments were being used to address economic concerns about the loss of key technologies to China.[13]

Much of the battle is one for control of global standards, an enormous source of revenue. The multinationals owning key patents incorporated in global standards, for example in communications, receive billions of dollars in royalties each year, including in China. As China became an electronics manufacturing center, newspaper headlines screamed about license fees paid to owners of the European GSM and American CDMA telecom standards patents. The Chinese government estimated that the percentage of fees to foreign companies on wholesale prices constituted 20 per cent of handsets, 30 per cent of computers and 20–40 per cent of machine tools. Chinese DVD player makers claimed they paid $10 in royalties for each product they sold for about $30.[14]

There is no way to enter the global market without adopting the standards everyone else is using, so there is no alternative to paying for them—unless one develops new standards and manages to get them widely accepted. This is where the Belt and Road comes in. "The return on investment for a port in Sri Lanka or a rail line in Thailand matters less to Chinese officials than the ability to push participating countries to adopt Chinese standards on everything from construction to finance to data management." China is already highly successful in exporting key technical standards for the construction of high-speed rail, circumventing those set a long time ago by Western players and putting in place guaranteed streams of revenue. "To the extent that China's standards supplant Western ones, it will represent a direct threat to the profitability of non-Chinese companies."[15]

It is indeed a high stakes battle, as the case of fifth generation mobile communications technology perfectly illustrates. In the second half of 2016, the body that decides global standards for mobile data held three meetings with the goal of agreeing on a particular standard, the Enhanced Mobile Broadband coding scheme. After the Chinese computer manufacturer Lenovo voted to adopt a standard led by American firm Qualcomm rather than a Huawei alternative, its founder Liu Chuanzhi, was forced to explain the seeming break with national unity and loyalty.

Remarkably, Liu revealed he had spoken to Huawei founder Ren Zhengfei, who confirmed he had no issues with Lenovo. "We both agree that Chinese companies should be united and must not be provoked by outsiders," he added, before speaking about his company's efforts over the past thirty years and expressing zero tolerance for any questioning of the loyalty of the "national brand." The dispute highlights how much national champions are expected to benefit from the definition of which technologies will be used to power the coming revolution in autonomous cars and the internet of things.

* * *

Because Germany's top firms have become so dependent on the Chinese market, the government in Berlin has avoided confronting China head-on.[16] The United States took longer to react, but when it finally did the response was considerably more aggressive. The ongoing dispute was initially centered around the country's trade deficit with China but quickly turned to Made in China 2025. The confrontation started on April 3, 2018 with the US proposing 25 per cent in added duties on roughly 1,300 Chinese products, such as industrial robots and other machinery. This would impact $50 billion, or 10 per cent, of total US imports from China. The determination claimed that China uses foreign ownership restrictions, such as joint venture requirements and foreign equity limitations, to require or pressure technology transfer from US companies and that its regime of technology regulations forces US companies seeking to license technologies to Chinese entities to do so on non-market-based terms that favor Chinese recipients. The list of products covered by the proposed tariffs was obtained from those benefiting from Chinese industrial policies, including Made in China 2025.

China responded the next day with its own plans for 25 per cent tariffs on 106 American products, including soybeans, automobiles and aircraft, that would also impact about $50 billion of imports from America. In the April 5 statement threatening more tariffs, President Donald Trump stressed that "the United States is still prepared to have discussions" with China. Neither country said when the duties would kick in, but Chinese government officials commented privately that Beijing would be unwilling to negotiate with the United States on any curbs on Made in China 2025. Unsurprisingly, China perceives the American demands as an attempt to stop China's economic development and technological progress.

"President Trump has made it clear we must insist on fair and reciprocal trade with China and strictly enforce our laws against unfair trade. This requires taking effective action to confront China over its state-led efforts to force, strong-arm, and even steal US technology and intellectual property," said US Trade Representative Ambassador Lighthizer. "Years of talking about these problems with China has not worked. The United States is committed to using all available tools to respond to China's unfair, market-distorting behavior. China's unprecedented and unfair trade practices are a serious challenge not just to the United States, but to our allies and partners around the world." The Chinese government's technology transfer and intellectual property policies are part of China's stated intention of seizing economic leadership in advanced technology as set forth in its industrial plans, such as "Made in China 2025."[17]

In May 2018 a high-level US delegation was sent to Beijing to negotiate the terms of a grand bargain. The draft agreement provided by the American side in advance of the visit—never made public—included a clause mandating that China would immediately "cease providing market-distorting subsidies and other types of government support that can contribute to the creation or maintenance of excess capacity in the industries targeted by the Made in China 2025 industrial plan." China said "big differences" remained as the US government delegation headed home. "There's no space for negotiation on China's development," said Ruan Zongze, executive vice president at Beijing's China Institute of International Studies, a think tank affiliated with the Foreign Ministry. "China has to progress, and it's unstoppable by anyone."

The shock waves from this clashing rhetoric were already being felt all over the world. In one of the most extraordinary examples reported at the time, a ship carrying sorghum, loaded with the grain in Texas and bound for Shanghai, suddenly performed a U-turn in the Indian Ocean when China announced a 179 per cent tariff on imports of sorghum. The vessel's destination was changed to Cartagena, Spain, but according to imaging data, it never docked. On May 18, as a provisional deal between the two trade giants seemed in sight, China scrapped its anti-dumping and anti-subsidy probe into sorghum. The same day, the *RB Eden* began sailing back across Gibraltar, bound for Singapore.

At the end of May the US government announced it would move to implement previously threatened tariffs after June 15, with Beijing quickly promising to reciprocate. US commerce secretary Wilbur Ross and vice premier Liu He did not issue a joint statement after they wrapped up two days of discussions in Beijing. The previous round of talks, held in Washington two weeks earlier, ended with only vague promises by Chinese officials to reduce their country's trade surplus with the US. The focus of the Beijing discussions was exclusively on narrowing the trade deficit, with a particular focus on energy exports.

As announced, the opening salvoes of the trade war were launched on July 6, with 25 per cent tariffs on $34 billion in Chinese goods being applied at midnight, followed by another $16 billion two weeks later. China retaliated with measures of equal magnitude that took effect as soon as it confirmed the US had indeed fired the first shot. "The Chinese side, having vowed not to fire the first shot, was forced to stage counter-attacks to protect the core national interests and interests of its people," the Chinese Commerce Ministry said in a statement. "The United States has started the largest trade war in economic history." Censorship instructions, issued to the media by government authorities and subsequently leaked, were more explicit: "The trade conflict is really a war against China's rise, to see who has the greater stamina. This is absolutely no time for irresolution or reticence." The same instructions placed a ban on further use of Made in China 2025: the plan had set off alarms bells in the United States and contributed to turn much of the American foreign policy establishment against China. President Trump raised the stakes, threatening to extend levies to all $500 billion of goods imported from China in a blunt outline of his plans to escalate the fight.

Just as in May, a ship—this time carrying soybeans—gave a less abstract image of the developments. *Peak Pegasus* was expected to arrive in Dalian on July 6, the same day that China was to impose its retaliatory tariffs on imports from the US. Since China is twelve hours ahead of Washington, the cargo had to reach Dalian before noon local time to beat the tariffs. Internet users in China offered encouragement and support to the cargo, which had left Seattle on June 8, a month earlier, as it became uncertain whether it would dock and unload its cargo before noon. It did so at 17:30, missing the deadline by just a few hours.

On September 17, 2018, President Trump announced a second phase of additional tariffs on roughly $200 billion of imports from China, set at a level of 10 per cent until the end of the year but expected to rise to 25 per cent after January 1. The statement from the White House again described the tariffs as a response to practices and policies deemed a grave threat to American economic interests—practices that China showed no willingness to change. Any hopes of an agreement were quickly receding, even as the two economies started to show signs of stress from the ongoing confrontation.

A trade war is particularly dangerous for China because it risks impairing the very engine of its remarkable economic success in recent decades: China's centrality in global manufacturing value chains. With value added in China making up only a small percentage of the final price, tariffs can have a crippling impact, making it unprofitable for global companies to locate production stages in China, especially final assemblage, which are far more vulnerable to tariffs. And since one of the most immediate and ineluctable results of a tariffs war is a decline in China's exports and foreign exchange income, an initiative as ambitious as the Belt and Road will become increasingly hard to finance.[18]

* * *

No doubt China could have access to commodities extracted in developing countries or the technology from developed nations without the Belt and Road, but the process would be subject to the normal operation of market mechanisms. What the Belt and Road does is increase China's control over the way value chains are organized and grant it the power to reorganize them on better terms. To give the most obvious example, the Chinese economy still has to rely on a steady supply of foreign-made semiconductors, the heartbeat of the internet of things and the industrial factories of the future, a fragility made evident when the giant electronics company ZTE was taken to the brink of extinction after the Trump administration temporarily banned it from buying US-made components such as chips. In a speech two years earlier, Xi Jinping had berated China's dependence on foreign suppliers for critical components and key technologies.

The concept of power is central to the global value chain approach. After all, if the value chain is not organized from above, it is just a set of more or less episodic market relations. In reality, we find that value chains operate according to strict parameters, enforced by what the academic literature calls "lead firms," who undertake the functional integration and coordination of internationally dispersed tasks. Other actors or firms in the chain must follow their guidance, as in the case when large global retailers control the production of agricultural products in the developing world, even when they do not own the farms or the packing facilities. These retailers tend to take ownership of the product only when it arrives at the regional distribution centers in Europe or the United States, but that does not stop them from controlling what happens at earlier points in the chain.

Lead firms derive their power from a combination of factors that can include their dominance in retail markets, their easy access to capital, their ownership of brand names, and their command and control over critical technologies. These firms are thus able to shape global value chains, control the locations of production and the distribution of value throughout the chain and directly affect the position of other actors along the chain. This is not contradicted by the fact that lead firms often delegate part of the organizing function to key suppliers, who take on the role of orchestrating flows of products, capital, managers and supervisors, and in some cases workers, across diverse production locations across the globe and increasingly shape the geography of the global value chain.

One of the easiest ways to understand how global value chains denote relations of power that tend to operate outside the sphere of political relations is to note that the opening up of markets and the removal of trade barriers is often immaterial for producers in developing countries, who can export to North America and Western Europe only to the extent that they gain access to the lead firms in global value chains. For them it is less a question of entering Western markets than of entering Western-led value chains.

Control over the full extension of the value chain multiplies the power that can be exercised at each stage. For example, it is because China now sits on a large portion of the shipping value chain—from building a ship all the way until it calls at the port—that it is increasingly able to command better deal terms and wrestle contracts from more established firms. When a French carrier recently placed an order for nine large container ships at Chinese yards—reputedly worth $1.5 billion—it was understood that they picked China over South Korea in large part because the deal included attractive rights to operate piers and containers at some of the large network of ports built and controlled by Chinese companies. It is by leveraging the full power of the value chain, starting from infrastructure, that Chinese shipping yards are moving upwards to more sophisticated vessels and not just simple bulk carriers, which have thus far been the country's staple. Ports form part of the strategic network that controls supply chains. Control over a port means power over which ships get priority in allocation of berths and port services. In times of conflict, this could include the power to block ships.[19]

The United States and Europe have benefited enormously from being home to some of the lead firms in global value chains. Now they face a number of difficult questions. First, many American and European multinationals may see their supply networks erode as China emerges as a rival buyer and producer. For example, China has already replaced France as the importer of choice for timber from Gabon. In time, important countries in European-led value chains may be recruited for Chinese-led rivals. Second, Western companies may find themselves directly competing with China in high-value markets, especially if China can organize its own global networks, and losing important streams of revenue from controlling the standards used worldwide. Finally, the United States and Europe face a third variable, one that is not primarily about the losses they will incur when Chinese companies start to be better represented in high-value segments of production. The principal issue is what set of rules will govern the way these value chains are organized.

The Chinese model is to conduct this organizing process as much as possible at the political level, through agreements reached directly between national governments. If we take the case of the automobile industry—the best example of an industry radically transformed by the global value chains revolution—the prevalence of joint ventures may indicate a unique developmental model, in which foreign and Chinese automakers cooperate in building highly efficient value chains. Joint ventures are legal partnerships between a domestic firm and a foreign investor to form a new operation in the domestic market and typically involve widespread use of proprietary technologies, intellectual property, and advanced production methods. This model was extremely successful in China, less so elsewhere. To gain a foothold in an overseas market, international automakers generally prefer direct exports, or to set up wholly-owned corporations. The establishment of joint ventures has often been a compromise for the foreign firms, and indicates strong negotiating power on the part of the host country—in this case China—which sees it as a way to force technology transfers. In other words, China deliberately avoided both the Mexican and the Korean models of subordination to large foreign firms or autonomous national development, opting to integrate its automobile industry in global value chains while preserving control over the process. Revealingly, in China enterprises owned by the central government all set up international joint ventures, while national carmakers are all private companies.[20]

The Belt and Road takes this strategy one step further. Hu Huaibang, Chairman of the China Development Bank, has argued that the most important goal of the Belt and Road is to help China undergo economic structural reform and upgrade its industries, moving away from a cheap, mass manufacturing model: "On the one hand, we should gradually migrate our low-end manufacturing to other countries and take pressure off industries that suffer from an excess capacity problem. At the same time, we should support industries such as construction engineering, high-speed rail, electricity generation, machinery building and telecommunications to compete abroad."[21] The explicit goal is to support what Chinese decision makers call "international capacity cooperation." The countries along the Belt and Road have different resource endowments and strong economic complementarities. The key to the success of the initiative is to make use of comparative advantage. Most of the countries along the Belt and Road are in the early stage of industrialization and have insufficient funds, while advanced economies are in the late industrialization stage and specialize in high-end technology. China is the Middle Kingdom. It has entered the middle period of industrialization, but its sheer size and financial clout make it an exceptional case. Financial cooperation under the Belt and Road framework can leverage China's capital and capital strengths and promote the use of capital to promote "capacity cooperation" and optimize the distribution of global value chains. As Jin Qi, Chairman of the Silk Road Fund, put it, "financial support should be the main driving force for international capacity cooperation."[22]

A document prepared by the National Development and Reform Commission and the China Development Bank—never made public and the subject of wild speculation—gives a clear sense of the scale and ambition of the Belt and Road in Pakistan, arguably the country where the initiative is moving faster. The plan envisages a deep and broad penetration of almost all sectors of Pakistan's economy by Chinese companies and its wholesale reorganization to fit with Chinese-led value chains. "With a decrease in the workforce and increase in labor costs in China, its manufacturing industry has to handle key problems in transformation and upgrading. However, the demographic dividends of Pakistan provide an important basis for development of the manufacturing and service sectors. Chinese manufacturing enterprises relocate their factories to Pakistan for lower labor costs and greater internationalization. This also promotes the upgrade and reconstruction of the manufacturing industry of Pakistan and creates many employment opportunities for the local people."[23] A key element is the development of new industrial parks, surrounded by the necessary infrastructure and a supporting policy environment. Chinese plans for Pakistan are focused on agriculture and low-tech industry, advancing a pattern of specialization where China can move into higher-value sectors and segments. It is only in agriculture that the plan outlines the establishment of entire value chains in Pakistan, including the provision of seeds and pesticides. The favored steering mechanism is credit, with those companies interested in the agriculture sector being offered free capital and loans from the Chinese government and the China Development Bank.

Ten key areas for engagement in the agriculture sector are identified along with seventeen specific projects. They include the construction of one NPK fertilizer plant as a starting point "with an annual output of 800,000 tons". Meat processing plants in Sukkur are planned with annual output of 200,000 tons per year, and two demonstration plants processing 200,000 tons of milk per year. In crops, demonstration projects of more than 6,500 acres will be set up for high yield seeds and irrigation, mostly in Punjab. In transport and storage, the plan aims to build "a nationwide logistics network, and enlarge the warehousing and distribution network between major cities of Pakistan" with a focus on grains, vegetables and fruits. Storage bases will be built in Islamabad and Gwadar in the first phase, then

Karachi, Lahore and another in Gwadar in the second phase, and between 2026–2030, Karachi, Lahore and Peshawar will each see another storage base. In 2015, China imported $160 billion worth of agricultural products. Pakistan's share in these exports was minuscule—less than half a percentage point—despite having a large agrarian base and a shared border with China. The Belt and Road will change this, but if agriculture becomes a central plank of the initiative in Pakistan that cannot but raise concerns about premature deindustrialization.

The plan also shows interest in the textiles industry, but its focus is in yarn and coarse cloth, which can serve as inputs for the higher-value segments of the garments sector being developed in Xinjiang. It is suggested that some of the Chinese surplus labour force could move to Pakistan, while the establishment of international value chains is described as the model of "introducing foreign capital and establishing domestic connections as a crossover of West and East." This seems to be a reference to the West's model of investing in China as a way to make its value chains more competitive, a model that the Chinese authorities will now attempt to replicate in Pakistan.

Xinjiang has become one of the most competitive and rapidly developing textile zones in China, even compared with Vietnam and other regions of Southeast Asia. The industry output value is planned to increase from 30 billion yuan in 2014 to 400 billion yuan in 2023. Xinjiang is the nearest region of China to Europe with the shortest and most cost effective transport time: an international freight train through Xinjiang takes only twelve days to reach Germany. The overall equipment performance of the Xinjiang textile industry is relatively high. The equipment of leading enterprises has reached an advanced level, and key equipment such as blowing-carding machinery, combing machines, automatic winders and shuttle-less looms have a higher utilization rate than China's national average. Thus "China can make the most of the Pakistani market in cheap raw materials to develop the textiles and garments industry and help soak up surplus labor forces in Kashgar to develop the city into an industry cluster area integrating textiles, printing and dyeing, cloth weaving and garment processing." By 2023, Xinjiang will become the largest cotton textile industry base of China and the most important clothing export base in Western China. The largest city, Urumqi, will turn into the fashion capital of Central Asia.

Finally, fibre-optic connectivity between China and Pakistan will prepare the ground for new digital television services disseminating Chinese culture, and electronic monitoring and control systems ensuring the security of the project. The safe city project will deploy explosive detectors and scanners to cover major roads and crowded places in urban areas to conduct real-time monitoring. The plan envisages a terrestrial cable across the Khunjerab pass to Islamabad, and a submarine landing station in Gwadar, linked to Sukkur. From there, the backbone will link the two in Islamabad, as well as all major cities in Pakistan. China's telecom services to Africa need to be rerouted in Europe, a "hidden security danger" or a digital version of the Malacca dilemma—Western powers could block traffic or use it for intelligence gathering—which new links through Pakistan will eliminate. Huawei is installing the Pakistan-East Africa Cable Express, which will connect Gwadar to China's new military base in Djibouti by 2019. The project has a total length of 13,000 km and will connect South Asia and East Africa, with a northern expansion to Egypt and further southern expansion from Kenya to South Africa.

Both governments set up a joint working group "to supervise and promote the implementation of major projects, to provide background support, to regularly discuss project progress, to address challenges that may be encountered, and to put forward coping strategies." Remarkably for a plan prepared by a Chinese government agency and a Chinese development bank, "it is suggested that Pakistan adopt the government-led mode of development." This means that the government makes an investment in building industrial parks and attempts to integrate all government functions in some industry cluster areas, and establishes unified but relatively independent government regulatory agencies to take overall charge of all affairs concerning industrial areas and financing as well as part of the administrative functions of local governments, and introduce industrial development projects through policy support, tax preference, investment promotion and land transfer. The public and private sectors have different roles, with the government setting the pace and direction for the initiative but leaving most practical details to individual companies. As we discussed in a previous chapter, finance holds the structure together: "International business cooperation with Pakistan should be conducted mainly with the government as a support, the banks as intermediary agents and enterprises as the mainstay. First, it is necessary to give full play to the government's influence, establish good relationships with local banks and businesses. Second, overall business objectives can best be achieved by giving full play to local banks' advantages in market knowledge and local enterprises' operating conditions, to provide loans in various forms, such as credit grants and syndicated loans, and other financial services."

* * *

"International industrial capacity cooperation" is China's way of preserving state guidance in a globalized world. Different countries cooperate on the basis of their comparative advantage and patterns of specialization, but without renouncing the ability to guide the economy in particular directions using a broad array of policy tools. That this does not result in robust economic nationalism and protectionism is predicated on the creation of platforms for widespread cooperation in the development of national economic strategies. One could say that under the Belt and Road, countries open their policy-making processes to other countries before and above opening their economies to foreign companies. For example, in 2018 China asked Kyrgyzstan to export 400,000 tons of honey, a task the Head of the State Inspectorate for Veterinary and Phytosanitary Safety described as unfeasible (the annual world output of honey in 2016 was 1.79 million metric tons). More detailed negotiations are expected to follow.

The initiative and final strategic vision always lies with Beijing. In Kazakhstan, to give another example, Chinese companies and the Chinese state have invested in the development of industrial clusters intended to sell titanium dioxide, silicon dioxide and vanadium pentoxide to China for use in the aircraft and aerospace industries. Recent industrial projects include Kazakhstan Aluminum, the Kaz Minerals copper mine in Aktogay, and Petrochina's petcoke project in Pavlodar, all of which are at least partly funded by Beijing's policy banks, China Development Bank and the Export-Import Bank of China. These are part of the fifty joint Kazakhstan-China industrial capacity cooperation projects agreed in 2015, worth $25–30 billion over five years, and intended to create industrial cluster cooperation zones in transport infrastructure, manufacturing, construction, and agriculture.

Reciprocal investments in China, on the other hand, continue to be limited, with Chinese authorities blocking every attempt by Kazakh conglomerates to raise capital on the Shanghai or Hong Kong stock markets. Capital must be used in ways that further China's industrial transformation and should not be squandered elsewhere. Interestingly, these same conglomerates are encouraged to work with Chinese companies in third countries. Eurasian Resources Group, a Kazakh company, has partnered with China Nonferrous Metals Industry Group, Export-Import Bank of China, Industrial and Commercial Bank of China and

China Export & Credit Insurance Corp to complete an $800 million copper and cobalt project in the Democratic Republic of Congo's Katanga district. The project came online in 2018 to supply China with 20,000 tons of cobalt, its single biggest supplier, enough to make batteries for 500,000 electric vehicles.

Kazakhstan's 'bright path', '100 concrete steps' and 'strategy 2050' industrial policies have been planned to intersect with China's industrial plans since the outset of the Belt and Road in 2013. In Central Asia, many states retain partially functioning or unclosed industrial complementarity loops, a heritage of their position as peripheral nodes in the Soviet continent-wide state industrial planning. Present-day water resources, transport networks, energy networks, and a variety of traditional industrial bases remain dysfunctional or isolated due to the economic decoupling from Moscow. Thus China is well positioned to move into the empty space and reactivate the old reciprocal links.[24]

The economic geography bringing all these projects together is one where the Congo occupies the bottom segments of the supply chain, Kazakhstan moves to the middle and China occupies the top, reserving for itself both the most lucrative segments of production and the organizing role. Western companies are— in this case—nowhere to be seen.

4

THE BELT AND ROAD AND WORLD POLITICS

Commander Kulbhushan Jadhav, now condemned to death by a Pakistani military court, had an uneventful childhood as a police officer's son growing up in Mumbai. He burst onto the national and international limelight in 2016 when Pakistan announced the arrest of an alleged Research and Analysis Wing (R&AW) Indian spy in its restive Balochistan province. Officials released a spliced and edited tape in which Jadhav is seen confessing to having been a spy for more than a decade. Recruited by R&AW in 2013, he had since been directing various activities in Balochistan and Karachi at the behest of the Indian intelligence agency with a view to engaging Baloch separatists to target infrastructure work on the China-Pakistan Economic Corridor.

According to the taped confession, Jadhav was trying to cross into Pakistan from the Saravan border in Iran on March 3, 2016, when he was captured by the Pakistani authorities. The Pakistani Army claims he used an Indian passport under an assumed name, Hussein Mubarak Patel.

"His goal was to disrupt development of the China-Pakistan Economic Corridor (CPEC), with Gwadar port as a special target," Pakistan Army chief Qamar Javed Bajwa said, adding, "This is nothing short of state-sponsored terrorism. There can be no clearer evidence of Indian interference in Pakistan." The Indian government categorically denied the allegations.

In late 2016 several scholars from my think tank at Renmin University in Beijing, the Chongyang Institute for Financial Studies, traveled to Pakistan on a field trip along the China-Pakistan Economic Corridor, during which they investigated the events surrounding the Jadhav arrest. In a report published soon after, they claimed that Jadhav secretly infiltrated Pakistan's Balochistan province at the end of 2013. Operating under the code name "Monkey", his main activities in Pakistan were to penetrate the Balochistan nationalist party and deliberately increase Pakistan's internal conflicts and divisions over the construction of the China-Pakistan Economic Corridor, to liaise with Baloch separatists and terrorists and to fund terrorist activities and provide combat training for insurgents in activities that undermine Pakistani law and order. The main targets were Gwadar and Karachi.[1]

The report went on to provide some context for the Jadhav spy story. India believes that the China-Pakistan Economic Corridor is a major threat to its national security. Not only will China's military power appear simultaneously in its east, north and west flanks, but Pakistan will also be able to completely cut off India from Iran. The Arabian Sea and Central Asia provide access to oil and gas energy sources, increasingly under China's control. It is a high stakes game but—the Renmin University report concluded—India's strategy to deal with Pakistan is not limited to a destructive one. In late May 2016, Indian Prime Minister Narendra Modi visited Iran. As the most important outcome of this trip, India will invest $500 million to build Chabahar Port in the province of Sistan-Baluchistan in the southeast of Iran, a direct rival and competitor to China's flagship project in Gwadar. The port allows India to bypass Pakistan and reach land-locked Afghanistan and Central Asia. India, Iran and Afghanistan have signed an agreement to grant preferential treatment and tariff reductions at Chabahar to Indian goods headed toward Central Asia and Afghanistan and the first consignment of wheat from India to Afghanistan was sent via Chabahar in October 2017.

* * *

In June 2017 Chinese troops were spotted extending a road through a strip of land disputed between China and Bhutan. India perceived this as an unacceptable change to the status quo and crossed its own border—in this case a perfectly settled one—to block those works. The Doklam plateau slopes down to the Siliguri Corridor, a narrow strip of Indian territory dividing the Indian mainland from its North Eastern states. Were China able to block off the corridor it would isolate India's North Eastern region from the rest of the country, a devastating scenario in the event of war.

Colonel Vinayak Bhat served in the Indian Army for over thirty years. He was a satellite imagery analyst, stationed in high altitude areas, where he also attended border personnel meetings as a Mandarin interpreter. I asked him why he thought Beijing was so determined to establish control over the Doklam plateau. After all, these border areas are far removed from any population center, and in many cases the actual border is difficult to determine—the demarcation goes back to old treaties between the Qing Empire and the British Raj and outdated, hand-drawn maps. Does it matter who gains an advantage here? "It matters," Bhat told me emphatically. "If the Chinese control Doklam, especially South Doklam, they will be able to threaten the Siliguri Corridor. After the Doklam plateau it will all be downhill. You need anything from nine to sixteen battalions in these high altitude mountains for each defensive battalion. So that changes the calculations."

The Doklam standoff ended with a choreographed disengagement on August 28. India agreed to withdraw its troops in a designated two hour period before noon and the Chinese did the same in a similar window that afternoon. The withdrawal was monitored from New Delhi in real time. By agreeing to discontinue construction works on the road, China seems to have met India more than half way, but it also used the occasion to state that it would exercise its sovereign rights in the future. More than a resolution of the crisis, the negotiation was meant to avert the risk of an accidental conflict. Troops from both countries remain in the area, but are now separated by a few hundred meters. Indian Army Chief Bipin Rawat quickly warned, "As far as the Northern adversary is concerned, flexing of muscles has started. Salami slicing, taking over territory in a very gradual manner, testing our limits or threshold is something we have to be wary about. Remain prepared for situations that are emerging gradually into conflict."

India's rejection of the Belt and Road may have triggered the confrontation that developed later in the summer. One month before the Doklam standoff, China had gathered about thirty national leaders at its first summit devoted to provide guidance for the Belt and Road. India announced just one day before the event that it would not be participating, explaining that in its current form the Belt and Road will create unsustainable burdens of debt, while one of its segments, the economic corridor linking China and Pakistan, goes through the disputed areas of Gilgit and Baltistan in Pakistan-occupied Kashmir and therefore ignores Indian core concerns on sovereignty and territorial integrity. A statement released on May 13, 2017 by India's Ministry of External Affairs explained: "We are of firm belief that connectivity initiatives must be based on universally recognized international norms, good governance, rule of law, openness, transparency and equality. Connectivity initiatives must follow principles of financial responsibility to avoid projects that would create unsustainable debt burden for communities; balanced ecological and environmental protection and preservation standards; transparent assessment of project costs; and skill and technology transfer to help long term running and maintenance of the assets created by local communities." The journalist Ashok Malik from the *Times of India* called the boycott the third most significant decision in the history of Indian foreign policy, after the 1971 decision to back the independence of Bangladesh and the 1998 nuclear tests.

"China would never force any country to participate in the Belt and Road initiative if it was too skeptical and nervous to do so," an article in the Chinese state-run *Global Times* quickly responded. "It is regrettable but not a problem that India still maintains its strong opposition to the Belt and Road, even though China has repeatedly said its position on the Kashmir dispute would not change because of the CPEC."

The truth of the matter is that the Belt and Road poses a number of seemingly intractable challenges for India. Most obviously, it threatens to turn Pakistan's occupation of part of Kashmir into a fait accompli. If the area becomes an important economic corridor for China, the conflict is no longer capable of being resolved within the limited sphere of relations between Pakistan and its much larger neighbor. Just before the May 2017 summit Beijing made one last effort to convince India to attend. In a speech in Delhi, its ambassador to India floated the idea of renaming the China-Pakistan Economic Corridor. The suggestion was that the new name would no longer imply that the economic corridor ran only through the two countries, implicitly denying Indian claims to territory occupied by Pakistan. Left unsaid was what the new name might be and how it might avoid raising objections in

Pakistan. Indian authorities never took the suggestion very seriously anyway, convinced as they are that the problems raised by the Belt and Road and its segment in Pakistan have more to do with increased Chinese presence than purely symbolic matters. When I asked Subramanian Swamy, a leading figure in the ruling Bharatiya Janata Party, how his infatuation with the project of dividing Pakistan in four was compatible with his warm feelings towards China, he answered that India would be able to convince China that a war between India and Pakistan would not interfere with the Belt and Road. I was not persuaded.

Economically, the challenge is, if anything, even graver. As a major economy hoping to remain on a trajectory of fast economic growth, India needs to develop deep international links and supply chains, most immediately in its neighborhood, but the Belt and Road may well force it into new forms of economic isolation, this time involuntary, as opposed to the years of Indian economic autarchy. New Delhi may even see in the Belt and Road a form of rewriting history by rebuilding trade and economic links between Europe and Asia while ignoring the Indian subcontinent, historically a meeting point for such trade and cultural networks.

The view from Beijing is just as cynical. While India remains for the time being a much weaker economy and state, it seems to have the forces of the future on its side. Chinese commentators have grown comfortable comparing China's economic vigor with the slow decay of the ruling powers in Europe and North America. This mental framework has made conflict improbable, since China feels time is decisively on its side. With respect to India the power equation is examined in a different way. Perhaps China will be inclined to act against a rival if the relation of forces can only deteriorate in coming decades. Naturally cautious, Chinese state media outlets have not avoided talking openly about the possibility of a war with India. That China and India are growing strong simultaneously is an entirely new fact, one carrying significant risks.

Certain economic anxieties play into this dynamic. As China's economic growth is tabling out, and slowing down as the numbers of young people in its work force dwindle, India will jostle for the place of global economic success story with its rewards in international prestige and investment flows. Its advantages correlate directly with China's weaknesses: the demographic dividend of a young population—even if that young population also poses serious challenges—and a public culture much more comfortable with experimentation and the exposure to different cultural influences. Its information technology strength continues to rival that of China.

If we limit ourselves to measures of economic or military power, China's edge is obvious, but things look very different when we turn to that most elusive of power metrics: soft power, the ability to project your way of life abroad and attract global audiences. The West's superiority in this area is still so massive that China and India are forced to compete for a limited space. India is winning. Bolstered by its familiarity with the English language and the freedoms granted by a democratic society committed to some version of the rule of law, the Indian cultural and entertainment industries have captured global attention in ways that China can only dream about. More worryingly for Beijing perhaps, they have started to appeal to Chinese audiences and to do so under the radar of Chinese anti-Western control mechanisms. Appearing in movie theaters just before the Doklam standoff, the Bollywood movie *Dangal* collected over $190 million at the Chinese box office, capturing the imagination of viewers young and old with an uplifting story of female empowerment and the collective pursuit of happiness—better, presumably, than anything produced in China.

Given Buddhism's religious and cultural influence in a vast area stretching from Mongolia to Japan and Southeast Asia, it is hardly a surprise that China and India have increasingly been trying to use it as a diplomatic tool. In the process they have often clashed in their attempts to conquer the hearts of Buddhists in Asia and exert power over different sects, their rites and procedures for reincarnation and enthronement. As China translates its economic power into a form of spiritual might, rebuilding monasteries and pilgrim routes, while creating psychological links with the people of other nations through Buddhism, India is forced to accept that even in this area the rules of great power rivalry increasingly apply. The Dalai Lama is inextricably linked with the border dispute between the two Asian giants. The Tawang monastery's historical ties to Tibetan Buddhism is an important basis of China's claim to Arunachal Pradesh, which lies to the south of the McMahon Line, the border originally drawn up by the British. China seems to consider that it will only be able to fully subdue Tibet after it annexes Tawang, where the next Dalai Lama may well be reincarnated.

A description of the role of Tibetan Buddhism within the Belt and Road has been put forward by Wang Changyu, Party secretary at the High-level Tibetan Academy of Buddhism. The Academy's experience training Tibetan Buddhist monks and its well-developed system of scholarly degrees creates an advantageous position allowing it to "help countries and territories along the 'Belt and Road' satisfy their demand for religious specialists and scriptures." Such exchanges can serve two goals: to showcase "the results of our Party and country's ethnic and religious policies, displaying the healthy heritage and development of Tibetan Buddhism" in China, while reducing "the Dalai clique's space of activity, upholding national sovereignty."[2]

Ultimately India constitutes a special challenge to Chinese expansion because, as a separate civilization tracing its origins to the same axial age five millennia ago, it cannot be assimilated into the expanding Chinese orbit in Asia. Frank Moraes recalled in his book, *Witness to an Era*, how when he went to China as a member of India's first cultural mission to the People's Republic in 1952, Nehru briefed the delegation before they departed: "Never forget the basic challenge in South-East Asia is between India and China. That challenge runs along the spine of Asia". What was true then remains the case today, but the rivalry between the two countries for leadership in Asia has expanded as their status rose and has acquired today a markedly global significance. The rivalry has also been ideologically refined, as countries in the neighborhood and beyond watch the contest between Delhi and Beijing to see which political and economic system comes out on top.

The standoff at the Doklam plateau was also the occasion for new tensions affecting trade relations between the two countries. In response to China's incursion in the Himalayas, India approved antidumping procedures against a number of Chinese imports and a planned takeover worth more than $1 billion by China's Shanghai Fosun Pharmaceutical of Indian drugmaker, Gland Pharma, was delayed. Doklam provided a pretext, but India is also growing fearful of ceding control over strategic industries to China. After reports that Chinese smartphone companies are sending user data of Indians to China, the Indian government started cracking down on these companies. The next step would be to require Chinese handset makers to set up servers in India to ensure the protection of user data. China responded to the standoff in similar tones: an ambitious high speed train project in south India was delayed after the Chinese railways that completed a feasibility study a year before suddenly stopped responding to the Indian ministry's contacts.

These moves could not hide how dependent the Indian economy has become on imports from China. Local manufacturing companies in India are not geared up to supply goods to the rising power and telecom sectors, so in the case of an open trade war India might be forced to import such components from the United States and Europe at prohibitive cost, destroying its own export competitiveness. Meanwhile Indian goods continue to struggle to find markets in China. The trade gap between the two countries has grown inexorably in recent years, reaching a staggering $51.1 billion in the most recent year on record. That this needs to be redressed is clear, but the path to greater Indian competitiveness will only shrink as economic and trade dependency on China extends more generally. It is not surprising that New Delhi is aggressively trying to create a more balanced relationship and an obvious area where this could be achieved is pharmaceuticals. Many Chinese patients travel to India to find drugs they desperately need but are either unaffordable or unavailable in China. Notably, China does not allow imports of drugs from India, even as Indian companies have become one of the dominant global players. Indeed China has lately been trying to pose a direct challenge to Indian drug-makers. Of the roughly 170,000 drugs approved by the China Food and Drug Administration, over 95 per cent are generics, according to the country's National Health Commission. In April 2018, the government of China issued a new policy package—including tax breaks—to promote the manufacture of generic drugs. China's aggressive presence in the market for generic drugs is now palpable. For instance, India's largest drug-maker, Sun Pharmaceuticals, reported a 75 per cent plunge in its third-quarter net profit for 2017–18 as it has been battling increased competition in the generics market from China. Far from reducing tensions, trade is becoming its own source of conflict between China and India, with every protectionist measure triggering a swift and more serious retaliation from the other side.

Until recently these tensions might be regarded as little more than peripheral skirmishes, but as the Chinese and Indian economies have grown in size and global economic integration has deepened, they are now highly dependent on each other and, together, represent a critical percentage of global economic growth. Whether the two governments are able to reach a stable economic order, and which form it will take, cannot but dramatically impact the rest of the world. Their rivalry is no longer a strictly Asian affair.

Calculating the global economy's center of gravity—the average location of economic activity measured on a globe across different geographies—provides further clues to what is going on. In the three decades after 1945 this was located somewhere in the middle of the Atlantic, reflecting how Europe and North America concentrated a large majority of global economic activity. That Washington saw itself as leading a bloc encompassing the Atlantic is, from an economic point of view, what you would expect. By the turn of the century, however, the center of gravity had shifted so far eastwards it was now located east of the borders of the European Union. Within ten years we should find it on the border between Europe and Asia, and by the middle of this century most likely somewhere between India and China, on the roof of the world.

An open struggle for mastery between China and India may never materialize, but as a latent conflict it is already one of the most important variables in world politics. It brings different trends and forces together. It was perhaps always to be expected that India would emerge as the main obstacle to Chinese expansion. That role may yet strengthen or dilute, but it is difficult to see it disappearing in the near future. More likely, those who are growing concerned about Chinese power will increasingly place their bets on India as a first point of contact, a power-balancer. To this fact China itself will be forced to respond, bringing the tectonic clash closer to the surface of world politics.

* * *

The 2018 National Defense Strategy of the United States opens by describing a strategic environment of growing competition with revisionist powers. Revealingly, the first example is how China is using its military and economic power to coerce neighboring countries to reorder the "Indo-Pacific region" to its advantage. China, it adds, is pursuing "Indo-Pacific hegemony." Later the document stresses the capacity to deploy military force in three key regions. Two of them are, unsurprisingly, Europe and the Middle East. The third—and in fact the first one mentioned in this context—is the Indo-Pacific.

Our mental maps are being redrawn. One of the most striking examples of this is the new concept of the Indo-Pacific. The first thing to note is that it signals an extension, an enlargement of the orbit within which actors operate. As often in the history of geopolitics, the concept was originally employed by biologists aware that marine life in the Pacific and Indian oceans formed a single continuum and that borders were an obstacle to scientific work. Geopolitical thinkers have slowly come to the same conclusion. Can political and economic questions be addressed within the confines of a narrow definition of the Western Pacific or the Indian Ocean? Or should we attempt to combine the two areas in a larger geopolitical unit? The answer should never be taken for granted, but many recent developments point towards the need to think in terms of larger and larger units, and these larger units—as opposed to the limit case of the whole planet—are not abstractions but practical considerations for the actors involved.

What gives force to the concept of the Indo-Pacific is first of all the expanding role of China and India on the global stage. Seen from the traditional centers of political power in Europe and North America, it is still tempting to think of China as an East Asian nation and of India as a South Asian nation, but we know that this now flies in the face of reality. For two decades China has been extending its influence and activities to the Indian

Ocean. It has invested in ports in Sri Lanka and Pakistan, sent its submarines across the Malacca Strait with increasing frequency and even—in the most dramatic instance of this overall development—opened its first overseas military base in Djibouti at the other end of the Indian Ocean. More recently this expansionism has been given a catchy name: the Maritime Silk Road.

India has followed suit, albeit more slowly, reflecting the gap in the historical development of the two countries and the ten or fifteen extra years it took New Delhi to understand that economic autarchy was an idea whose time had passed. What happened then was that India started to realize that, if China was increasingly present in its own backyard, perhaps the inverse movement had become necessary. At first this may have looked like a pure game of power. How to prevent China from abusing its newly found presence in the Indian Ocean without developing corresponding leverage points in the Western Pacific? Far from surprising, a decision to do so was always inevitable, and merely reproduced dynamics of mutual pressure and influence the countries have become used to along their land borders and peripheral regions in Kashmir, Tibet, the Northeast and the Himalayas.

More substantial concerns quickly emerged. First, trade and economic development. We have grown so used to think of India and China as the two economic giants in Asia that we forget there is a third pole of development which, in the aggregate, may turn out to be just as significant. What is more, both India and China are discovering that in a world of deepening economic integration and transnational value chains, their development is closely linked to Southeast Asia, where opportunities for trade, infrastructure investment and sourcing abound. What should India do? By turning west it would face the stagnant or turbulent Middle East or then the mature European economies. By turning east it can find ample ground for investment and booming trade relations with Indonesia, Malaysia, Vietnam and the Philippines.

New Delhi certainly thinks that it cannot abandon Southeast Asia, with its unmatched economic potential, to Chinese economic interests if the relation between the two countries is to preserve, over the long term, the promise of an eventual balance and parity. This brings us to an equally important point: the economic and trade links between China and India and the physical infrastructure of transport and communications needed to support them. The economic links between the two countries are bound to dominate the world economy by the middle of the century. Should India leave the development of this network of economic links to China? It seems far more prudent to ensure from the very start that this will be a collective project, pregnant with rivalry but where both countries can have a major stake.

Finally, there is the question of Japan. India increasingly sees Japan as its primary source of technology. The symbiotic relationship between an aging technological powerhouse and a young country still on the path of industrialization cannot be missed. In return, Japan sees in the Indian navy an indispensable partner in its efforts to contain Chinese expansion and safeguard freedom of navigation in the East and South China seas. Both countries know that they will find in each other a receptive ear when expressing concerns about the rising threats to the Asian maritime commons. It is no coincidence that the concept of the Indo-Pacific first saw the light of day during a 2007 visit by Prime Minister Shinzo Abe to India, where he spoke about the "confluence of two seas." In the spring and summer of 2007, the Indian navy sailed all the way up to Vladivostok, the home port of the Russian Pacific Fleet, and conducted a series of bilateral and multilateral exercises with the United States, Japan, Russia, and China.

There is a page in K.M. Panikkar's *India and the Indian Ocean*—a book published in 1945—where the great strategic thinker seems to discover the Indo-Pacific, like a navigator crossing a far-flung strait. He noted that the strategic position of the Indian Ocean had dramatically changed since the nineteenth century. Then all that mattered was the connection to the Atlantic and—after Suez—the Mediterranean. Japan's lightening conquest of Singapore and the Bay of Bengal showed that the Indian Ocean could be controlled from the east and Japan's defeat would not be able to put the genie back in the bottle, not least because China would in the future have even more advantages than Japan. The connection that would increasingly matter was that between the Indian and the Pacific.

The Indo-Pacific as a concept of political geography is neutral, objective. Every actor is coming to the realization that it needs to act in this extended sphere or, in other words, that its objectives in a more limited area cannot be pursued within that area alone. China and India may be more directly implicated in the change of perspective, but it affects an external actor like the United States no less powerfully, for instance when it realizes that it is better able to develop a coherent policy towards China and India if it thinks of the two together as part of the same system.

Nevertheless, this is no more than the beginning of the story. Although every actor shares an understanding of the Indo-Pacific as a single system, their understandings are to some extent mutually exclusive. When the United States speaks of the Indo-Pacific as a space of freedom managed by a condominium of India, America, Australia and Japan, this is not only a project very different from China's Maritime Silk Road, but may in fact be defined in opposition to it. What these four countries seem to share, what separates them from other democracies in the region, is a deepening suspicion of Chinese plans.

It is here that we come face to face with the most singular and important fact about contemporary geopolitics: political and economic integration, the dilution of borders, goes together with increasing competition about how this enlarged space is to be managed and defined. That one of the great civilizational borders existing today is being slowly removed should not be underplayed. We have only to think how difficult a similar process would be on the other end of the Eurasian supercontinent to realize this. Consider how momentous a transformation it would look to us if Europe and the Middle East were thought of as a single unit. It is a process of that kind that we are watching along the Asian littoral arc as the border between East and South Asia—a border which has in the past stopped whole armies in their tracks—is being questioned, doubted and perhaps, in the end, forgotten.

The Indo-Pacific thus appears as a test case of wider processes of Eurasian integration. To a considerable extent, sharp divides between regions of the kind we have been discussing have their root in the age of European colonial empires. They sometimes originated in the competition for territory and areas of influence between rival European powers. In other cases, they followed from the administrative imperative of each of these powers, which found it convenient to organize their territories in separate units. Often these divisions were superimposed on older and more permanent racial or religious divides, but European colonial power did much to reinforce them or even create them where they had a very incomplete meaning. Different regions in Asia were connected to the center in Europe in such a formalized way that relations among themselves could not be directly established but had to pass through the center, which worked as a hub assigning and distributing culture, ideas and money to the regions. Much more fundamental than the borders between these different regions, the division between region and center was the organizing principle of the whole system.

At the beginning of the twentieth century, as the age of European empires seemed to be coming to an end, visionary authors such as Halford Mackinder or Alfred Mahan started to advocate the idea of a Eurasian supercontinent from which these modern divisions had been removed. Unknown to them, a new age of divisions—ideological rather than cultural or political— would then follow, but this was perhaps no more than the last breath of the clash between European civilization and a world caught up in the throes of modernization. In our time we have returned to the question of Eurasia with renewed vigor. Major actors such as India or China outgrow their historical boundaries. Civilizational borders seem less fixed, more fragile than we thought and, perhaps unsurprisingly, the process is developing much faster in the former imperial regions, whose borders were less central to the system, than in the borderlands between Europe and Asia. East, Southeast, South Asia. As the regions dissolve, Eurasia coheres.

The Indo-Pacific is the central stage where the new system is being rehearsed. As Raja Mohan put it, the Indo-Pacific forms the great connecting arc delimiting Eurasia in all directions and Eurasia might best be seen as the hinterland of the Indo-Pacific.[3] That, in the final analysis, explains why China sees a strategic threat in the very concept of the Indo-Pacific. Understood as a geographic concept it merely repeats ideas conceptualized by Beijing in the context of the Belt and Road, but the same underlying reality carries different—opposed—political meanings. The term "Indo-Pacific" is less the acknowledgment of an ineluctable political geography than an initial, inchoate move to create a political initiative, one intended to rival China's Belt and Road.

Australia, the United States, India and Japan are discussing the creation of a joint regional infrastructure scheme as an alternative to the Belt and Road. The four countries have recently revived their informal arrangement to deepen security cooperation, a decade after the Quadrilateral Security Dialogue—also known as the Quad—first met. The next step would be to grant it an economic dimension. Offering a contrast to the Belt and Road, a readout of the meeting of the Quad held on the margins of the ASEAN summit in Manila in November 2017 noted that officials discussed "increasing connectivity consistent with international law and standards, based on prudent lending," and would enhance coordination on this and other issues "to further strengthen the rules-based order in the Indo-Pacific region."

Many remain skeptical. As the former Australian foreign minister Bob Carr put it, a working definition of the Belt and Road is that China is exporting a surplus in infrastructure to its neighbors. Now, India has no such surplus capacity and its 800 million voters might want to sweep from power any government that tipped funds to build infrastructure abroad. As for the US, it cannot boast a single kilometer of high-speed railway to rival China's 25,000 km.[4] According to Josh Rogin, a *Washington Post* columnist, the Chinese believe America and its partners have no economic and financial capacity to compete with Beijing's multi-trillion-dollar Belt and Road, so they are little concerned with US complaints about it.[5]

On July 30, 2018, speaking at the newly created Indo-Pacific Business Forum, Secretary of State Pompeo announced that US business engagement would be at the center of the Trump administration's strategy for advancing a free and open Indo-Pacific. He continued: "So just as the United States made foundational contributions in the past, today I am announcing $113 million in new US initiatives to support foundational areas of the future: digital economy, energy, and infrastructure. These funds represent just a down payment on a new era in US economic commitment to peace and prosperity in the Indo-Pacific region." The announcement might be seen as a turning point—from an exclusive focus on security to economic development—but the funds committed to the effort were paltry, especially when compared to the trillion-dollar Belt and Road. The infrastructure pillar of the initiative is seeded with a mere $30 million.

Pompeo quickly explained that values are more important than money: "With American companies, citizens around the world know that what you see is what you get: honest contracts, honest terms, and no need for off-the-books mischief." In response, Chinese Foreign Minister Wang Yi commented: "The US is the sole superpower in today's world, with a GDP totaling $16 trillion. So when I first heard this figure of $113 million I thought I heard wrong. At least it should be 10 times higher, for a superpower with $16 trillion of GDP."

In a meeting at the State Department in Washington in September 2018 the official in charge of coordinating the US's response to the Belt and Road was dismissive of Wang's humor. The new funds, he told me, consisted merely of added money to development assistance in one fiscal year. They would swiftly be followed by parallel initiatives, such as a new bill that would boost the US's role in international development. It would combine several little-known government agencies into a new body, with authority to do $60 billion in development financing—more than double the cap of the current agency that performs that function—while lifting the current prohibition on owning equity in projects. The latter change was meant to allow the United States to work more closely with investment agencies in countries such as Japan.

* * *

Speaking at the Center for Strategic and International Studies before his first visit to India in October 2017, then Secretary of State Rex Tillerson argued that "we need to collaborate with India to ensure that the Indo-Pacific is increasingly a place of peace, stability and growing prosperity so that it does not become a region of disorder, conflict, and predatory economics." Asked to elaborate on that comment during the questions period, he added: "We have watched the activities and actions of others in the region, in particular China, and the financing mechanisms it brings to many of these countries, which result in saddling them with enormous levels of debt. They don't often create the jobs, which infrastructure projects should be tremendous job creators in these economies, but too often foreign workers are brought in to execute these infrastructure projects. Financing is structured in a way that makes it very difficult for them to obtain future financing and oftentimes has very subtle triggers in the financing that results in financing default and the conversion of debt to equity. So this is not a structure that supports the future growth of these countries."

One of his final acts before leaving the State Department was to warn his hosts during a visit to several African nations that "China offers the appearance of an attractive path to development, but in reality" participants in the Belt and Road are "trading short-term gains for long-term dependency." Further revealing comments on the initiative came from Secretary of Defense James Mattis during a hearing before the Senate Armed Services Committee in October 2017: "Regarding 'One Belt, One Road,' I think in a globalized world, there are many belts and many roads, and no one nation should put itself into a position of dictating 'One Belt, One Road.' That said, the 'One Belt, One Road' also goes through disputed territory, and I think that in itself shows the vulnerability of trying to establish that sort of a dictate." And in August 2018, we finally found out what President Donald Trump personally thinks of the Belt and Road. According to one person sitting in the room, he told a group of business executives gathered at his Bedminster golf club that Chinese President Xi Jinping's "One Belt One Road Initiative," was "insulting" and that he did not want it. Trump said he had told Xi as much to his face.[6]

A pivotal consequence of the Belt and Road has been to force the United States to adopt a similar concept of geographic space.

Hence the adoption of the Indo-Pacific concept, but as Tillerson made clear in the last six months of his tenure, the geographic concept needed to acquire a normative meaning before being put to use. The Indo-Pacific became "the concept of the Free and Open Indo-Pacific Strategy." By introducing those two modifiers, Washington wanted to push back against the notion that Western values are doomed to lose influence in the core regions of the Belt and Road. It also wanted to engage India more directly in its reaffirmation of liberal values. India is invested in a free and open order. It is a democracy. It is a nation that can boost and anchor the "free and open order" in the Indo-Pacific region, and American power will increasingly try to ensure that India plays that role and becomes over time a more influential player in the region.

After several years during which the Belt and Road was perceived in Washington as a relatively modest project of economic diplomacy, the initiative has steadily grown in status and is now regarded as a major strategic threat to American power. Two areas of analysis have been developed in parallel. On the one hand, the ways in which the Belt and Road directly targets a US-led global order have been articulated. On the other, a strategy to contain and disrupt the initiative is slowly being implemented. Washington has started to appeal to countries it deems of strategic importance in order to establish how they can become less vulnerable to Chinese influence. Many of these countries are deeply divided in their views on the Belt and Road. Predictably, China and the United States will have their own privileged audiences. The two countries will be supporting different elements within the elites and political class, attempting to help them prevail in the domestic competition for power. There is much here to remind us of the Cold War, including the presence of an increasingly visible military element.

In his Senate confirmation hearing in April 2018, the new commander of the US Pacific Command, Admiral Phil Davidson, was asked about his assessment of the military and strategic implications of the Belt and Road. Davidson was surprisingly outspoken, expressing no doubts or reservations about a military reading of the initiative. "The predatory nature of many of the loans and initiatives associated with the Belt and Road Initiative," he explained, "lead me to believe that Beijing is using the Belt and Road as a mechanism to coerce states into greater access and influence for China." When participant countries are unable to pay back these loans, Beijing offers to swap debt for equity. As a result the Chinese military could gain access to air and military port facilities, perhaps even pressuring nations into denying American forces basing, transit and operational and logistic support. China claims that "the Belt and Road Initiative will not be used for military means, but their words do not match their actions." After Davidson's appointment, the Pentagon announced a new name for the Pacific Command, with a change to Indo-Pacific Command meant to "better encapsulate the responsibilities the command currently has."

It was no coincidence that Davidson's comments were made when General Wei Fenghe, Chinese state councilor and defense minister, met with the visiting Pakistani Naval Chief of Staff Admiral Zafar Mahmood Abbasi in Beijing. According to reports in the Chinese media, Wei told his guest that China will work with Pakistan to focus on building a community of shared future for mankind, consolidate all-weather friendship, deepen pragmatic cooperation in various fields between the two armed forces, and provide strong security guarantees for the joint building of the "Belt and Road Initiative." For the first time the intention to provide the Belt and Road with "security guarantees" was publicly voiced. Abbasi, in turn, expressed his congratulations on the world-renowned achievements made by the Chinese armed forces. He said that Pakistan highly cherishes the traditional friendship with China and is willing to continuously deepen exchanges and cooperation between the two militaries in high-level exchanges, military training and technology, to promote the continuous and in-depth development of relations between the two countries and the two militaries.

Along the land corridors included in the Belt, security concerns have always been paramount. Many of the countries in Central Asia present more or less latent threats from Islamist terrorism and militancy. In fact, to the extent that it promotes new connections, the Belt and Road may turn out to exacerbate these threats. As Chinese economic interests penetrate more deeply into the local economies, feelings of Sinophobia may be expected to grow. Direct security risks to China became visible when a car bomb exploded after ramming the gates of the Chinese Embassy in Bishkek in August 2016. Uncertain political transitions and persistent territorial disputes create another set of concerns. The role played by both Kyrgyzstan and Tajikistan as transit states for the narcotics trade from Afghanistan is problematic for China, which is an end market for such drugs. In Pakistan many of the connectivity projects pass through troubled areas, including Balochistan, where an armed insurgency remains active. In September 2016 reports suggested that two Chinese engineers had been killed by militants while working on the Dudher Zinc project in Hub district, Balochistan. In December 2017 the Chinese Embassy in Islamabad said on its website that it had information about a "series of terror attacks" planned against Chinese organizations and personnel, without giving details. A Chinese man working with a shipping company in Pakistan was shot dead in February 2018 in what police described as a targeted attack in Karachi.

In some cases we have been able to find out more about these personal stories. They reveal surprising patterns of cultural contact and expansion, with all the attendant risks, a new world of connections being shaped by the Belt and Road. In June 2017, for example, a pair of young Chinese nationals was executed by the Islamic State in Pakistan after being kidnapped from Jinnah Town. They had been living in Quetta since their arrival in the country on a multiple entry business visa towards the end of 2016, part of a group of Chinese men and women brought to Pakistan by a Korean, ostensibly to learn Urdu and then teach the language to the other Chinese expected to arrive in the future. At first, it was thought that the motives might be commercial, as large numbers of Chinese workers and businessmen arrive in Pakistan each day and are greatly in need of translation services. During the investigation, the Pakistani police concluded that the Korean and the group of Chinese, including the victims, had violated the terms of their visas because they were involved in preaching Christianity.

Beijing is clearly worried that Islamic militants from the Middle East—or West Asia as the region is known in China—could cross Central Asia and enter Xinjiang province. In early 2018, several reports surfaced of a new Chinese military base in the Wakhan corridor in Afghanistan. According to Afghan officials, China and Kabul started discussing building a base in Badakhshan and China will send an expert delegation to Kabul to determine the exact site. China has denied these reports, but witnesses reported seeing Chinese and Afghan troops on joint patrols. There is a long record of signs of a growing Chinese military interest in Central Asia and the discussion about the potential establishment of permanent military bases can only become more intense.

One example that seems highly illustrative of the importance of the security dimension in the Belt and Road is that of Frontier Services Group, the security services firm founded by Erik Prince, former Blackwater chief, which is actively working with China on Belt and Road projects. The fact that the firm has been allowed to set up a forward operating base in Xinjiang and

Yunnan provinces shows it enjoys strong support from the highest levels of the Chinese security apparatus. Frontier says its trainers in China are unarmed and are not engaged in operations, only in passing along security skills. Prince told China's *Global Times* that Frontier will operate in the main "corridors of the One Belt and One Road initiative": "The Northwest corridor includes the countries of Kazakhstan, Uzbekistan, Pakistan, Afghanistan and the Southwest corridor includes Myanmar, Thailand, Laos and Cambodia." Following in Prince's footsteps, a Chinese soldier who served in the French Foreign Legion recently launched a recruitment drive to create an all-Chinese crew to serve as security for overseas Chinese companies, according to the *Chengdu Economic Daily*. Among his assignments in the Foreign Legion was a 4-month tour of Mali after the military coup destabilized the western African country in 2013. Wrapping up his service with the French Foreign Legion, Fu Chen has now registered a security company in his native Tianjin.

Faced with a growing number of threats to Belt and Road investments and projects, China may feel the need to increase its military presence in the region. The more assets, investments and citizens China has abroad, the more time it will have to spend on thinking strategically about their security, but any movement in this direction would dramatically change the nature of the Belt and Road, increasing different forms of resistance and opposition to the initiative, while risking a conflict with Russia, the dominant security agent in large parts of Central Asia, the Caucasus and the Middle East.

* * *

China may insist that the Belt and Road is a strictly economic project, but that is a claim bellied by its own efforts to promote the initiative. It ebbs and flows with the rhythm of political strategy, political thinking and political action. It does not follow the pattern of individual decisions by economic agents promoting their own interests, but obeys a national vision and relies on the tools of national power for its success. From the start, China made that success a measure of its political influence and made sure that all the power of the Chinese state was placed behind the initiative.

This, for better or worse, was how the rules of the game were defined. The first three years of the Belt and Road were still a period of reflection and exposition. Since then, power has become the organizing principle. Beijing pushes ahead, sometimes subtly, other times much more aggressively. Other countries have been forced to respond, either by joining the initiative or by devising a method to oppose it. Geopolitics has triumphed.

Blowback against the Belt and Road followed almost immediately upon its initial successes. As we saw above, opposition from the United States and India—with the two countries encouraging each other down that path—grew consistently throughout 2017. In 2018 the surprising winner in Malaysia's general election, Mahathir Mohamad, criticized Chinese projects for raising the country's debt without delivering significant benefits and promised to renegotiate the terms and do away with mega projects, in the process managing to destroy the image of Malaysia as the poster-child for the Belt and Road. He combined the message with an appeal to new infrastructure investments, but those did not seem to include the prized high-speed rail linking Kuala Lumpur to Singapore, the logic of which he questioned. Intriguingly, the claim that Malaysia gains nothing strategic from the high-speed rail connection could be interpreted to mean that Malaysia should not assist Singapore by funding infrastructure that assists a competitor in preserving and expanding its role as Eurasian trade hub, connecting to inland Chinese industrial and logistics centers.

Soon after the election, Mahathir said he had written a personal letter to Chinese President Xi Jinping suggesting an overland Silk Route. "As you know, when the demand for oil grew, ships were built bigger and bigger until they were almost half a million tonne, but trains have remained small, and not long enough. So I suggested to Xi Jinping in a personal letter to him, that we should have big trains, and China has the technology to build big trains, which can carry goods from China to Europe." The problem with the maritime section of the initiative became clearer when he added: "As far as the Belt and Road problem is concerned, we have no problem with that, except of course, we would not like to see too many warships in this area, because warships attract other warships, and this place may become tense because of the presence of warships." The plan, it seems, is to push the Belt and Road as far away from Malaysia as possible.

In May 2018, Luhut Pandjaitan, the Indonesian maritime affairs minister, described the Belt and Road as a "Chinese proposal," from which Jakarta should try to keep some distance: "We do not want to be controlled by the Belt and Road. We would like it to link to our maritime policy, of a global maritime fulcrum." Addressing a Delhi audience, Luhut suggested that the port of Sabang at the westernmost point of Indonesia and just 700 km from Indian territory could be leased to India. China's acknowledgement of Sabang's strategic value was reflected in a *Global Times* editorial, which reiterated the significance of the Malacca Strait to China's "economic and energy security" and warned of "disastrous consequences" if India develops Sabang into a strategic base. "If India really seeks military access to the strategic island of Sabang, it might wrongfully entrap itself into a strategic competition with China and eventually burn its own fingers. A misconception by India in terms of outbound investment is that it always sees China as a rival that it pits itself against. But this idea will get India nowhere because China always sees the big picture when seeking investment overseas and aims for reciprocity and mutual benefit."[7]

Thailand is taking the lead in creating a regional fund with its neighbors, Cambodia, Laos, Myanmar and Vietnam, to back infrastructure and other development projects and to lessen reliance on Chinese investment. In June 2018 the Vietnamese government requested the National Assembly to postpone the bill on Special Economic Zones, saying it needed more time to ensure that it meets the aspirations of both legislators and the public among concerns about the potential undermining of national security and violation of sovereignty if foreign investors, especially Chinese, are allowed to rent land for up to 99 years in these areas. Myanmar is now seeking to take on no new loans from China to complete the Kyaukpyu Special Economic Zone and would offer the developer no sovereign guarantees to mitigate risk if it does, according to the project's new chairman, U Set Aung. "Hence, the project will not force the Myanmar government to bear the debt burden," he said. China International Trust and Investment Corporation won the bid to develop the economic zone in 2015. The shareholders agreement struck under then-President Thein Sein gives China an 85 per cent stake in the project and Myanmar the rest. The new government, led by the National League for Democracy, has been trying to double Myanmar's stake to 30 per cent.

Australia and New Zealand, in the meantime, have been caught up in a vortex of suspicion and recrimination about what they increasingly see as illegitimate Chinese attempts to gain political influence inside the two countries. In September 2017, it was reported that Yang Jian, a leading member of parliament from the National Party in New Zealand, had a military intelligence background in China that he failed to disclose when he immigrated to New Zealand and that he has pursued close ties with the Communist Party in Beijing. Faced with similar cases of heavy-handed interventions in local politics, Australia approved a wide-ranging package of foreign interference laws designed to force new levels of disclosure from people acting for other countries. At the end of 2017 one of Australia's most prominent public intellectuals, Clive Hamilton, argued that the Chinese Communist Party was inserting "agents of influence" at all levels of Australian political life. Damagingly, the book containing his claims was initially cancelled by its publisher amid fears Beijing would bankroll endless legal suits against it.

These controversies were bound to contaminate public perceptions of the Belt and Road. Increasingly the view in Canberra and Auckland is that companies should feel free to participate in the initiative but any form of political support to the Belt and Road carries high risks and no potential rewards. New Zealand and Australia see themselves primarily as members of a Western community of liberal democracies. To become too close to the Belt and Road would sow confusion and, in the case of conflict, force them into the kinds of choices they have worked hard to avoid.

Early reactions in Delhi and Tokyo, once outliers in their skepticism of the Belt and Road, now appear closer to the norm. Collectively, these developments suggest the initiative may bring together China's competitors rather than dividing them. But the key question is whether converging reactions can be turned into a coordinated response and, of course, how China will respond in that scenario.[8]

* * *

So far China has shown considerable adaptability in the way it manages the process. It realized early on that it needed at least formal support from Russia and it succeeded in obtaining it. Having Russia on board gave Beijing the green light to develop the initiative in Central Asia, one of its privileged areas. In Pakistan support for the Belt and Road goes very deep across the whole political establishment. When Prime Minister Nawaz Sharif was forced to resign over corruption charges in 2017, many predicted that China would have to restart its Belt and Road efforts anew, but in fact not much seems to have changed. The initiative may have to be adapted to changes in Pakistan's political landscape—an election result bringing a new party and political program to power will call for corresponding changes— but by that very token it now appears as part of the permanent institutional structure of the country.

The case of India is considerably more delicate. At first, the Chinese authorities seem to have made the calculation that, once Russia had joined the initiative and many of the countries in South and Southeast Asia were fully committed to it, India would have no choice but to follow suit, leaving China in a position to dictate the terms. The gambit proved to be misguided. India felt it was being cornered and reacted by turning explicitly against the initiative. Public opinion in the country became familiar with the Belt and Road, but its views are overwhelmingly negative. What is worse, Delhi was able to influence other countries, most notably the United States, and bring them closer to its views.

For China to continue ignoring or dismissing India's interests and positions might turn out to be a gross miscalculation. As Raffaello Pantucci argues, India is in a position to create insurmountable difficulties for China as it strives to implement the Belt and Road in its more ambitious version. In the competition for global markets, Indian consumers offer a decisive prize for Chinese companies as they try to overcome their American and European rivals. Stability in Pakistan is of course impossible without a measure of cooperation from Delhi, so Beijing may end up regretting it if India and Pakistan continue on their downward spiral of mutual hostility. Nepal and Bangladesh will always find themselves tied to India thanks to cultural, ethnic, and historical affinities. The same is true of Sri Lanka and the Maldives. "The nations of South Asia, unlike their Central Asian counterparts, have a clear alternative on offer in India. This is the trump card that New Delhi could play against China. It is one that Beijing has failed to consider adequately."[9]

The swing state in the great contest between different integration projects is, of course, India. As Andrey Kortunov puts it, "without the participation of Delhi, or even more with resistance from the Indian leadership, neither the American nor the Chinese vision can be fully brought to fruition."[10] Without India, the United States might be able to preserve its pattern of alliances in Asia, but its ability to compete on the scale of the Belt and Road would collapse. As for China, it can hardly claim that its "community of shared destiny" represents the image of the future world order if India were aligned with an alternative vision. And thus we are led to the current situation, where India, aware if its central importance, is in no hurry to make its choice.

If the initial calculus had been wrong, China was nonetheless able quickly to correct course. In February 2018, in a move that surprised analysts, it stayed neutral as Pakistan was put back on an international terrorism financing grey list, three years after it was removed from it. In April, just ahead of Indian External Affairs Minister Sushma Swaraj's visit to China, Beijing proposed the building of an economic corridor between China, Nepal and India that would cover ports, railways, roads, aviation, electricity and communication. India has yet to offer any kind of formal support for the Belt and Road, but seems mollified in its approach. Any talk of working with the United States to establish a Belt and Road alternative has been downplayed. An April 2018 summit between Modi and Xi aimed to reset the relationship between the two countries and discussed the possibility of joint infrastructure development cooperation in Afghanistan, albeit likely outside of the Belt and Road framework. Shortly before Modi's meeting with President Xi, India excluded Australia from participating in the Malabar naval exercises. Later, on the margins of the Shanghai Cooperation Organization summit in June, the two leaders settled a dispute over the flood-prone Brahmaputra river that flows from Tibet to Bangladesh in a sign of growing cooperation between them.

The way different countries have been responding to the Belt and Road can be organized in a relatively simple matrix. First, participant countries. Some of them may be only potential and others may have been quite reluctant to open their economies to Chinese economic interests, but discussions have been held and agreements signed with what must now be close to a hundred countries. Second, geopolitical rivals. The United States has been excluded from the initiative on the plausible grounds that the Belt and Road is a direct challenge to American power. Views in Washington were once more or less indifferent, but it remains difficult to imagine that they could ever become positive or that we could see China and the United States working together on major global initiatives. The same may perhaps be said of Canada, which Chinese authorities tend to regard as an American political and economic dependency.

Between these two extremes, we find a number of interesting variations. India, as we have seen, is perhaps best interpreted as a country whose exact place in the scheme is yet to be determined. As for Japan, it offers the fascinating possibility of a country intent on being both in and out of the initiative. While actively involved in developing Belt and Road alternatives, Japan has signalled its willingness to cooperate with China in infrastructure and industrial projects in third countries. In May 2018, for example, government representatives of China, Japan and Thailand announced their intention to pursue business collaboration in the Eastern Economic Corridor, a special economic zone along Thailand's eastern seaboard which is being heavily promoted by the military junta. Another candidate project in Thailand is aimed at extending the Bangkok Mass Transit

System, which currently links Phaya Thai Station in central Bangkok with Suvarnabhumi Airport, to another airport in a suburb 50 kilometers distant. Finally, a project to construct a high-speed railway between Suvarnabhumi Airport and a city in the central part of Thailand is also under consideration. Japan and China held their first meeting in Beijing in September 2018 to discuss economic cooperation projects in third countries. The committee is headed by Hiroto Izumi, a special adviser to the prime minister on the Japanese side and Ning Jizhe, vice chairman of the National Development and Reform Commission, on the Chinese side.

Japanese Prime Minister Shinzo Abe, while addressing Japanese and Chinese executives in Tokyo in December 2017, alluded to the possibility of Japanese participation in the Belt and Road. "I believe Japan will be able to cooperate well with China, which has been putting forward its One Belt One Road initiative," he said. To oppose the Belt and Road is to embrace an economic and political confrontation with China for which Japan is hardly prepared. It might also be unnecessary, if the goal is to avoid increasing its dependency on China. One can benefit economically from having access to the Belt and Road, provided other alternatives are developed, thus ensuring China has no monopoly over the future networks of infrastructure and economic integration.

On 21 May 2015 Abe announced that his government, together with the Asian Development Bank will jointly provide approximately \$110 billion to support "quality" infrastructure investment in Asia over the next five years. The initiative, baptized "Partnership for Quality Infrastructure," is meant to compete directly with China's Belt and Road on the basis of a differentiating mark: while Chinese plans are seen to emphasize quantity and speed, Japan relies on higher standards, where these are understood to extend from accounting, financial planning and

procurement practices to the durability, environmental sustainability, and safety of the finished infrastructure projects. Finally,
appropriate terms and conditions of loans should be set in accordance with best practices and rules taking into account the repayment abilities of recipients. In 2016 the initiative was expanded
to provide up to $200 billion globally over five years. It remains
the only direct rival to the Belt and Road. Its dedicated projects
include the Mombasa Port development project in Kenya, the
Nacala port in Mozambique, the Mumbai-Ahmedabad high-
speed railway in India, the Thilawa special economic zone in
Myanmar, the Matarbari port and power station in Bangladesh,
and the digital grid project in Tanzania. It is part of Japan's strategy of ambiguity not to actively promote its projects, so they
often fly under the radar, although many actually exceed their
Chinese rivals in scale and ambition.

* * *

At the other end of the Eurasian supercontinent, the European
Union is if anything even more unsure about what to do about the
Belt and Road. Though the initial focus of the Belt and Road is
naturally on China's immediate periphery, Europe lies as its final
goal and main justification. That has been conjured by the very
reference to the ancient Silk Road, whose associations remind us
of the old trade networks linking the Atlantic to the Pacific.

In the first two years of the Belt and Road there was simply
no reaction from Europe and the initiative remained for the most
part unknown. That started to change in 2015. The EU-China
summit in June that year highlighted the mutual interest in
China's bold infrastructure projects. The European Union was at
that time busy implementing its own infrastructure investment
strategy, the Juncker plan, and hoped China could support it
with a significant contribution. During the years of the eurozone
crisis, China had played a stabilizing role in many of the coun-

tries most in need of inward investment flows. Unsurprisingly, there was much goodwill left. A Connectivity Platform was created to ensure that investment projects approved by both sides could benefit from the highest synergies and interoperability.

Many of the arguments heard in Brussels at the time underlined that China seemed to have converted to the European Union model. Was not the Belt and Road a variation of what the EU offered, a multilateral and multinational project of economic integration? And if that were the case, any meaningful strategy had to encourage those efforts. As an influential report put it in May 2016, "simply by embarking on broad, multilateral integration efforts, the Chinese and the Russians have chosen to compete on the EU's terrain. European policymakers need not fear cooperating with these initiatives." When it comes to economic integration projects, it concluded, no one can beat Europe, so "the EU should respond by absorbing these projects into an inclusive order, bounding the competition with cooperation, and making the competition about what the EU does best: negotiating the nitty-gritty of complex frameworks of cooperation that are the sinews of multinational integration."[11]

EU-Asia trade in goods is by far the most important flow axis in global trade, peaking at $1.8 trillion in 2013, consistently more than double Transpacific trade and as much as three times Transatlantic trade, depending on the years. This is all the more surprising as it is precisely along the Eurasian axis that obstacles and barriers to trade are most significant, from poor infrastructure to tariffs and other trade barriers. Eurasian and Transpacific policies are still much less friendly than Transatlantic policy, with almost twice as many protectionist announcements. Though the gap has narrowed, Eurasian trade links remain less developed than Transpacific ones, so the potential for growth is highest in Eurasia.[12] Europe acquires enormous significance for China in the exact sense that it offers a vision of great power relations that

Chinese policymakers wish could be made universal and whose dynamics they have tried to replicate in relations with the United States, knowing full well that this is impossible: a deep economic relationship supporting China in its rise to the zenith of the world economy without the ticking clock of a coming geopolitical conflict. The fact that legally and politically the relationship is in its earliest stages also promises that China can play the main role in its final definition.

The initiative was originally well received by Europeans. If there were clouds gathering on the horizon, they had to do with the so-called 16+1 format launched by China in 2011, an initiative aimed at intensifying and expanding cooperation with eleven EU member states and five Balkan countries in the fields of investment, transport, finance, science, education, and culture. From the outset it was feared that the group would make it difficult for the EU to reach common positions on China, a concern that has only grown since the first summit of the group in 2012 in Warsaw. One obvious case is Hungary, where Chinese support seems to have provided political capital to the Hungarian government during its recurrent clashes with Brussels. In 2014, while serving as Europe Minister in the Portuguese government, I had an exploratory conversation with Fu Ying, then China's deputy foreign minister, on whether Portugal would be interested in leading the creation of a second group of countries benefitting from a permanent cooperation platform with China: the 6+1, including Portugal, Spain, Italy, Malta, Cyprus and Greece. Although the idea came with a number of perks—Lisbon could hope to be the location for the inaugural meeting, like Warsaw in 2012—we concluded that China had most to gain from splintering the negotiating power of the combined EU. We abandoned the opportunity and the idea was also dropped by Beijing.

China has become ever more entrenched inside Europe and the question at present is whether and how European countries can regain some measure of control over the mechanisms of Chinese influence. As a recent report puts it, China remains convinced that it is Europe which stands at risk of leaving itself stranded in a world where even the United States may be moving away from the liberal world order. Increasingly isolated, the European Union will try to avoid conflict at all costs. Europe will have to come around to the essential goals and values of the Belt and Road or face isolation, not the reverse. As the initiative is gradually implemented, the EU's ability to shape it in a particular direction will tend to disappear.[13]

Geographically, the sixteen countries in Central and Eastern Europe with which China has been developing closer ties form the last link in the complex future network linking Asia and Europe. The focus on infrastructure shows that China considers Central and Eastern Europe a full part of the Belt and Road, that is, as part of a new Chinese order, while countries like Germany and France tend to be seen as guardians of the old order. Central and Eastern Europe offer a number of other attractive possibilities for China. Still deficient in basic infrastructure, they can be enticed by cheap Chinese loans; in return, they will be expected to convey China's views and interests in Brussels. Many of these economies have become deeply integrated with German-led value chains. Competition between China and advanced European economies will hinge on who can ultimately attract these smaller economies to their orbit.

In an interview with a weekly magazine in June 2017, Angela Merkel, the German Chancellor, said Europe ought to be wary about opening its markets to products that had been developed with public subsidies in China and should demand reciprocity on access to public tenders. China's economic might allows it to pressure weaker European Union members, she added, in what seemed a reference to a veto by Hungary and Greece of a European Union statement criticizing China's human rights record earlier that month. "Seen from Beijing, Europe is an Asian peninsula." That was the new rallying cry coming from Berlin: Europe now ran the risk of being reduced to peripheral status. Whether the danger should be addressed through greater engagement, retreat or confrontation remained unclear. In September 2017, Sigmar Gabriel, the German vice-chancellor and foreign minister, called on Beijing to respect the concept of "one Europe" adding: "If we do not succeed for example in developing a single strategy towards China, then China will succeed in dividing Europe." The words were intriguing. They seemed to contain a thinly veiled reference to the "one China policy," the principle that there is only one country of China, despite the fact that the government in Taiwan also carries that name. Gabriel was wading into dangerous waters.

In July 2016, Hungary and Greece fought hard to avoid a direct reference to Beijing in an EU statement about a court ruling that struck down China's legal claims in the South China Sea. In March 2017, Hungary derailed the EU's consensus by refusing to sign a joint letter denouncing the reported torture of detained lawyers in China. In June 2017, Greece blocked an EU statement at the UN Human Rights Council criticizing China's human rights record, which marked the first time the EU had failed to make a joint statement at the UN's top human rights body.[14] As a source in the Foreign Affairs Council told me in 2017, China had become the main obstacle to the regular workings of the body.

Since 2015, many EU member states kept developing privileged links to the Belt and Road. The bloc as a whole took a decidedly more lukewarm approach, which is hardly surprising. As the initiative acquired a more practical orientation and its impact started to be felt, it became abundantly clear that China expected to remain at the helm. That would always be difficult to accept for the European Union, with its own plans to shape the global regulatory order and imprint its own values and procedures outside its borders. The clash, when it arrived, had a marked technocratic character.

In early 2017 the European Commission triggered a probe into a planned 350 km high-speed railway between Belgrade and Budapest, a flagship scheme under the Belt and Road. European officials told the *Financial Times* that the investigation was assessing the financial viability of the $2.89 billion railway and looking into whether it had violated European Union laws stipulating that public tenders must be offered for large transport projects. No contract for the $1.8 billion Hungarian section of the railway appears to have been made public.[15]

Gathered in Beijing for the first Belt and Road summit in May 2017, European Union countries declined to sign a joint statement on trade, uncomfortable with its omission of social and environmental sustainability, as well as imperfect transparency requirements, particularly in the area of public tenders. At the summit China received widespread support for its proposals, so the European dissent stood out, even threatening to mar the overall success of the gathering. "We felt this language was going backwards" from what China had previously agreed to, said one European official, who suggested Beijing had drafted the statement to benefit Chinese companies in future Belt and Road contracts. "It's about selling their stuff," the official said.[16]

In the immediate aftermath of the clash, both sides tried to play down the difficulties, arguing that the joint statement had been presented too late in the talks, making it impossible for an inclusive solution to be found. That this was not the root of the problem was made abundantly clear by developments over the following year. European governments and business associations have a long track record of complaining about lack of market access in China. It was inevitable that the same concern would be applied to the Belt and Road, where Chinese authorities were creating a similar range of barriers and obstacles. Establishing an open and transparent market system is from this perspective the only way to ensure a level playing field where the same rules would be applied to Chinese and foreign companies and where they would have equal opportunities to bid for lucrative contracts along the Belt and Road.

In a report made public in April 2018, twenty-seven ambassadors from the EU—Hungary declined to participate—wrote that China wanted to shape globalization to suit its own interests. They warned that European companies could fail to win good contracts if China is not pushed into adhering to the European principles of transparency in public procurement, as well as environmental and social standards. Whenever European politicians travel to China nowadays they're put under pressure by their hosts to sign agreements for the joint expansion of the Silk Road. "This bilateral structure leads to an unequal distribution of power which China exploits," the report said.

In parallel, Chinese investments in Europe have acquired greater and greater salience in the effort to control China's influence and avoid Merkel's peninsular fate. Supporters of stricter investment screening claim that the EU is currently allowing China to take its liberal system for a ride. Concerns include the possibility that Chinese investors may benefit from Chinese subsidies that put them at an unfair advantage, or that they may be acting on behalf of Beijing to seek control of strategic technologies, with no transparency as to who is really behind these acquisitions and investments.[17]

Mostly at the initiative of the German and French governments, lawmakers in Brussels are finalizing legislation that will give national governments more discretion to review and authorize Chinese investments. While claiming that the EU's openness to foreign direct investment will not change, the new regulation argues that openness has to be accompanied by vigorous and effective policies to, on the one hand, open up other economies and ensure that everyone plays by the same rules, and, on the other hand, protect critical European assets against investment that would be detrimental to legitimate interests of the Union or its Member States. In determining whether a foreign direct investment may affect security or public order, Member States and the Commission should consider all relevant factors, including the effects on critical infrastructure, technologies, including key enabling technologies, and inputs which are essential for security or the maintenance of public order. In that regard, Member States and the Commission should also take into account whether a foreign investor is controlled directly or indirectly by the government of a third country, including through significant funding.

Placed against the matrix of possible responses to the Belt and Road, the European Union seems to offer a final variation. As opposed to the United States, the EU has neither the tools nor the disposition to enter a new great game of geopolitical confrontation. As opposed to Japan or India, it does not enjoy the tactical flexibility of changing its position with each new development. What the EU wants is to participate in the Belt and Road while sharing with China managerial responsibilities in the initiative. It is placed in the difficult position of not being able to oppose an international project of economic integration while being equally incapable of joining it as a mere participant. It feels a natural inclination to tell China how the initiative should be organized and led, even if those suggestions will never find a receptive ear in Beijing. As one European diplomat told me—the lack of awareness is extraordinary—the European Union can have a very positive "scrutinizing role" in the initiative.

In September 2018 the EU presented its long-awaited strategy on "connecting Europe and Asia," immediately billed by some as Europe's response to the Belt and Road. As expected, the document is eminently technocratic, offering vague commitments to diminish or eliminate technical obstacles to greater connectivity in such areas as aviation, ports, railway or internet regulation. No new funding lines were announced and the relevant sections make clear that Asia will not be a priority for EU international investment. The core of the new strategy is the renewed insistence that the prerequisites for businesses to develop and promote EU-Asia connectivity are a level playing field in terms of market access and foreign direct investments and fairness and transparency in public procurement. The principles of sustainable, comprehensive and international rules-based connectivity inform the strategy. Through this approach, the EU will enhance regulatory quality and allow companies to compete fairly against each other, drawing inspiration from its own internal market. The superiority of EU rules and solutions seems to be presented as self-evident, based on a sort of epistemological judgment, and in no need of being actively supported and promoted against powerful alternatives.

From the perspective of Brussels and the main European capitals, China must fulfill its declared aim of making the Belt and Road an open platform which adheres to market rules and international norms in order to deliver benefits for all and to encourage responsible economic behavior in third countries. In the long term, it is perhaps inevitable that the two sides will negotiate a broad free-trade agreement reducing the growing tensions between the two integration projects, but that day still lies very much in the future.

As the French President Emmanuel Macron put it during his first state visit to China in January 2018, "by definition, these roads can only be shared. If they are roads, they cannot be one-way." In practice that means that rules have to be balanced between the interests of all sides. "After all, the ancient Silk Roads were never only Chinese," Macron told an audience of academics, students and business people at the Daming Palace in Xian. "These roads cannot be those of a new hegemony, which would transform those that they cross into vassals."

THE WORLD AFTER THE BELT AND ROAD

Trees grow on buildings here, planted on the roof, sprouting from the balconies, hanging from the walls, and so they called it Forest City. Throughout mankind's history cities have been hacked out of the jungle or reclaimed by the jungle when their time was up. In Forest City, the jungle and the city co-exist as one—you know you have arrived when the trees take over. My hotel stands in the middle of an immense construction site. The buildings around, hundreds of them, bedecked with cranes like giant winged insects, keep rising. When the night falls, they keep rising. Sometimes a skyscraper will be finished in as little as a week.

There are other peculiarities about Forest City. Its inhabitants are just starting to move in, and they are almost all Chinese. Shop signs are written in Mandarin, and the restaurants serve food from Sichuan and Yunnan. But the city is being built in Malaysia, not China. Forest City offers an early glimpse at a world reshaped by China, a world built according to Chinese rules and furthering the goals of a Chinese civilization unhampered by national borders. Not the old China—but the China of the new science fiction being created by Chinese millennials. The world of Forest City resembles that of Chinese science fiction author Hao Jingfang's *Folding Beijing*—with a splash of Plato's *Republic*.

From the moment you arrive it is impossible to miss that there are four separate social strata in the city. First, the residents: wealthy Chinese from the mainland, who may be looking for a new life outside China or at least a safe haven protected from undesirable developments at home. Second, those providing them with professional services of all kinds, from health to education and entertainment. They tend to be Chinese, although in some cases—like in the posh preparatory school opening in August 2018—Europeans or Americans may be preferred. Third, the guardians: Nepalese security guards, polite and distant. Fourth, the workers: Bangladeshi and Indian, responsible for construction and cleaning.

The city's scale is hard to compute. There is a very large hotel and a shopping mall at the center. But the city is still growing, the buildings under construction are only a small portion of the whole island that will one day be reclaimed from the sea. And this island will be joined by three others in the near future, and then by an extension on land, bringing the total area of the city to about half the size of Manhattan. The first resident will move in August 2018. But in ten years close to a million people are expected to live here.

I take a walk on the beach. There are numerous warnings against swimming. Forest City sits on one of the busiest shipping lanes in the world, and the heavy construction is not helping keep the waters clean. Fishing boats have all disappeared, replaced by construction trucks parked on the sand. I walk all the way to the end of the artificial island. Across a narrow channel there is still an old mangrove and then in the distance the port of Tanjung Pelepas, one of the largest in Asia. Just a couple of miles across the Johor straits lies Singapore. On a good day you can drive from Forest City to the Lion City in less than half an hour. "When Shenzhen was just a jungle," a sales agent tells me, "no one would have bought a house there. But it was across from Hong Kong and now everyone wants a house in Shenzhen. So why not buy a house across from Singapore?"

Forest City is a $100 billion joint venture between China's giant homebuilding company Country Garden from Guangdong Province and the Sultan of Johor, the sovereign ruler of the Malaysian state where Forest City is rising. Forest City's sales representatives proudly advertise the links to power as a guarantee that the project has political support. And the Sultan—so fabulously wealthy he owns a gold Boeing 737—has indeed delivered. The problems the city will experience will likely come from the capital Kuala Lumpur, where the newly elected Prime Minister has compared Forest City to Singapore at the time of its establishment by the British—given away to foreigners in exchange for almost nothing.

The best image of the Belt and Road is not the trains crossing the Eurasian supercontinent, or the ports and industrial parks opening up along the way. It's the cities being built up from scratch. These are what will change the physical and human landscape of the planet, creating new ways of life, new ideas, new adventures.

This is where the real competition between states and between political models will happen. It is not about territory; the economy is what matters. Nor is it about who has the biggest companies; those can relocate or be disrupted. It's really about ecosystems: collections of companies, workers and consumers—clusters of culture, social life and economic activity. In other words: cities. And in Forest City, China is betting that those can be built as easily as a new app or a gadget.

I had flown to Malaysia from San Francisco, where I had met tech people who are thinking about how to build technologically optimized cities and realize the old dream of the founders of Google: "give us a city and put us in charge." They seem to regard it as the natural next step for those who have already mastered building social networks on the internet. And so, the race is on—between two Bay Areas in San Francisco and the Pearl River Delta.[1]

* * *

What will the world look like after the Belt and Road? In the first Belt and Road summit in 2017 Xi Jinping hailed it as the "project of the century." If all goes according to plan, the Belt and Road will change the shape of the world economy and world politics, returning us to a time when China occupied, if not the center, at least a central place in global networks. Many of the features of the contemporary world that we take for granted would change rather dramatically as a result, but every future scenario must start by seeking answers to two questions: will the Belt and Road succeed? And what does success mean in this context?

Among the most common and most plausible criticisms of the initiative—one that comes naturally to Western commentators— is that the very logic behind the Belt and Road encourages decision-makers and companies to take undue risks, moving too fast and neglecting concerns about the sustainability of investments whose final justification is after all strategic. Impatience might turn out to be the initiative's worst enemy. China needs to show that the Belt and Road can succeed. This is not just because of the needs of an avid domestic and international audience, but because of the very ambition of its objectives. As it needs to be propelled forward against mounting obstacles, success—especially early success—is its vital fuel. Like every grand political project, it is fighting against inertia and entropy and therefore its leaders are bound to become impatient. Impatience, however, brings with it great danger. We know from bargaining theory that the most impatient player will tend to lose out, and China has multiple, endless negotiating processes ahead. Impatience is also responsible for tunnel vision, the tendency to think that everything that is not essential can be done later and that every other goal should be sacrificed to the main project. One obvious example is the fate of China's state-owned companies. Return on equity fell by more than half over the last decade, but many of the political incentives to poor performance—pressure to accept investments or strike deals that make political but not business sense—will be reinforced by the Belt and Road, with Xi calling state-owned companies its "essential forces." And finally, impatience is a powerful incentive to make mistakes, to shoulder too many risks and to neglect negative outcomes.

We have seen in previous chapters how finance works as the hinge holding the initiative together, but that means finance also has the potential to become its weakest link. Just as subprime in the United States concentrated political and financial incentives without proper scrutiny, the Belt and Road could introduce massive distortions in how capital is allocated, with potentially devastating consequences for all the countries involved. According to the Institute for International Finance, between the fourth quarter of 2008 and the first quarter of 2018 China's gross debt exploded from 171 to 299 per cent of GDP. High leverage is the original sin that leads to risks in the market for foreign exchange, stocks, bonds, real estate and bank credit, but making the necessary changes will be difficult, particularly in a world populated by trade wars and grand geopolitical initiatives.

In recent months Chinese authorities have started to tighten reins on debt, with debt growth slowing to the lowest rate in more than a decade. These figures point to growing risks of a slowdown for the Chinese economy, but even if the risks are adequately managed, a sharp reduction in credit creation will interfere with the scope and ambition of many ongoing and projected Belt and Road activities. In June 2018 the *Financial Times* reported that China is scaling back investment in Ethiopia in the face of rising foreign exchange shortages. Business people, diplomats and bankers said Chinese entities were taking a "more cautious approach" to Ethiopia. "Current international conditions are very uncertain, with lots of economic risks and large fluctuations for interest rates in newly emerged markets," said Hu Xiaolian, the chairwoman of the Export-Import Bank of China at a forum that month. "Our enterprises and Belt and Road countries will face financing difficulties."[2]

As for participant countries, they too are struggling with exploding debt levels, and unsurprisingly the problem is graver in their case. After the new government in Malaysia announced it was reviewing Belt and Road projects and cancelling most of them in order to avoid bankruptcy, Myanmar said it was reviewing the $9 billion deep-water Kyaukpyu port development, a flagship Belt and Road project, over concerns it is too expensive and could fall under Beijing's control in case the country defaults on its debt. The amount of debt Myanmar would need to take on for its share of the project would be about $2 billion, or about 3 per cent of GDP. It may be too optimistic to assume that many of the countries in the core Belt and Road regions have the absorptive capacity needed to provide an outlet for as much capital investment as China plans to provide through the initiative. Above that level, capital investment would offer better returns in China, a simple calculus quickly affecting the economic logic of the new integration model.

Beijing thus finds itself in a bind. If it takes on the bulk of the financing costs for the Belt and Road, risks to its financial system may go into the red, but if it attempts to push those risks onto participant countries, it will ensure that investments become divisive political issues, poisoning relations between China and other countries. Already in many countries, as we saw before, the backlash against the initiative is visible and gaining momentum. Debt is a concern, but other criticisms have been voiced. Mahathir Mohamad, who went on to win the 2018 Malaysian elections, complained during the campaign that Forest City showed that Malaysia was giving its most valuable and beautiful lands to foreigners and that many of the projects financed by China brought no benefits to Malaysia since even workers were brought from the mainland. In September 2018 Mahathir took the dramatic step of announcing that foreigners will not be issued visas to live in Forest City. "They can buy the property, but we won't give them visas to come and live here," the Prime Minister told reporters after an event at the National Art Gallery, reported the *Malay Mail*.

In many places in South and Southeast Asia and elsewhere China is struggling with accusations of corruption, which have become part and parcel of the political cycle: politicians seen as close to Chinese positions are vulnerable to those accusations during vicious campaigns, almost always turning public opinion against China and its growing economic clout.[3] From Cambodia to Pakistan to the Maldives, all of which held elections in 2018, opposition forces are using Chinese-funded ventures to go after incumbent governments. The former president of the Cambodia National Rescue Party, the main opposition group that was dissolved with a controversial court ruling, tried to exploit Prime Minister's Hun Sen image as a China acolyte: "What Hun Sen is doing is in order for China to help protect his power. The Chinese are allowed to freely enter Cambodia, to take land, islands, beaches and mines."[4] Malaysia's new government has revealed a possible China connection in the explosive 1MDB scandal, linking the problems at the graft-tainted state investment fund to two Beijing-backed pipeline projects that cost more than $1 billion apiece. Then, in July 2018 President Maithripala Sirisena of Sri Lanka made the announcement of a fresh grant of 2 billion yuan at a ceremony marking the start of construction of a Chinese-funded kidney hospital in his home constituency of Polonnaruwa, 230 km from Colombo. "When the Chinese ambassador visited my house to fix the date for this ceremony, he said that Chinese President Xi Jinping sent me another gift," Sirisena told the gathering. "He has gifted 2 billion yuan to be utilized for any project of my wish. I'm going to hand over a proposal to the Chinese ambassador to build houses in all the electorates in the country," he added. The grant offer comes at a time when a Chinese firm is facing heavy criticism for allegedly financing the last election campaign of former President Mahinda Rajapaksa.[5] Going one step further, President Rodrigo Duterte of the Philippines revealed in May 2018 that China will ensure he is not ousted from power. "The assurances of Chinese President Xi Jinping were very encouraging. Eh nandyan iyan sila. 'We will not allow you to be taken out from your office, and we will not allow the Philippines to go to the dogs,'" Duterte explained during a ceremony attended by Filipino scientists.

Even in Pakistan—the crown jewel of the initiative—the authorities have fallen behind on payments for electricity from new Chinese power projects because of longstanding problems getting Pakistanis to pay their bills. The Belt and Road has certainly contributed to the balance of payments crisis. Raw materials are required to construct buildings, bridges and roads, and Pakistan has to bring in all of them from abroad. The same applies to heavy machinery, where Pakistan's imports are set to top $27 billion by 2021. Pakistan can pay for Chinese machinery with Chinese loans, but unfortunately these loans are due before the economic gains that will be used to pay for them are accrued. A bailout from the International Monetary Fund seems inevitable—and Pakistan has received an IMF bailout twelve times since 1988—but it would create a number of renewed difficulties for the China-Pakistan Economic Corridor, including strict restrictions on borrowing and spending and transparency requirements for existing Chinese loans and projects. "Deals like the Orange Line cannot be secret," said Chaudhry Fawad Hussain, spokesman for the main opposition Tehreek-e-Insaf party, in a reference to the new overhead railway in Lahore, financed and built by Chinese state-run companies. One civil servant in Islamabad told the *Financial Times*: "The Chinese are not keen on western institutions learning the minute details of financing of CPEC projects. An IMF program will require Pakistan to disclose the financial terms to its officials."[6]

Finally, in case of a bailout, the United States, the largest contributor to the IMF, would acquire a significant measure of influence over China's plans in Pakistan. Beijing does have enough sway to ensure that Pakistani authorities reject an international bailout program, but in that case China would have to shoulder the financial costs all by itself and essentially double down on its high-risk Pakistan bet. The Chinese embassy in Islamabad responded to reports about a connection between the Belt and Road and the debt crisis in Pakistan with a statement published on July 23, 2018. There it was argued that 42 per cent of Pakistan's foreign debt is owed to multilateral financial institutions, with Chinese preferential loans accounting for only 10 per cent of the total. "Even if there is a debt trap," the statement concluded, "the initiator is not China." Adding to the complexity, the United States quickly started to have doubts about whether an IMF bailout was such a good idea after all. Secretary of State Mike Pompeo warned in August that any potential IMF bailout for Pakistan's new government should not provide funds to pay off Chinese lenders.

After the victory of Tehreek-e-Insaf in the July 2018 elections, the new Prime Minister, the former cricketer Imran Khan, seemed keen on a reset on the Belt and Road. His victory speech included these closely scrutinized lines: "China gives us a huge opportunity through CPEC, to use it and drive investment into Pakistan. We want to learn from China how they brought 700 million people out of poverty. The other thing we can learn from China is the measures they have taken against corruption, how they have arrested more than 400 ministers there." The phase after the elections will help define the ultimate fate of the Belt and Road in Pakistan. If the new Khan government demonstrates its willingness and capacity to focus on a serious economic reform and investment program, there is still an opening to address the mounting problems with the China-Pakistan Economic Corridor, which China does not believe to be insurmountable. Privately, the Chinese side has also made it clear that there is scope to renegotiate the terms of some of the ongoing or planned projects if it makes political and economic sense to do so.

If Beijing sees an extended period of political infighting, with a weakened government, distracted by religious and ideological propaganda, if as Andrew Small argues it has to navigate another round of bad press surrounding the Belt and Road, Beijing may well feel inclined to conclude that "Pakistan is unable to channel the requisite energy into making a success of their flagship connectivity endeavor."[7] In September 2018, a report by the *Financial Times* suggested that Pakistan might follow Malaysia in attempting to revise the terms of its participation in the Belt and Road, which Minister Abdul Razak Dawood—the Pakistani member of cabinet responsible for commerce, textiles, industry and investment—described as unfair, insufficiently thought through and disadvantageous to local companies. The report was swiftly attacked by Chinese and Pakistani authorities.

In April 2018 the IMF's managing director, Christine Lagarde summed up these concerns when she warned Chinese policymakers in a conference in Beijing to beware of financing unneeded and unsustainable projects in countries with heavy debt burdens. In an otherwise supportive speech on the Belt and Road, she noted the initiative's "ventures can also lead to a problematic increase in debt, potentially limiting other spending as debt service rises, and creating balance of payments challenges." Echoing Western complaints about insider dealing—especially acute for the European Union—she added that "with any large-scale spending there is sometimes the temptation to take advantage of the selection and bidding process."

In April 2018 the *Financial Times* published an editorial arguing that the Belt and Road "is an accident waiting to happen." So what should Beijing do? "China needs to take a responsible approach to its role as a creditor. That does not mean it should be excessively risk averse. To lend for development is, quite properly, to take risk. But it is also to assess projects and fiscal positions rigorously and, when things go wrong, share in the losses, without imposing unduly onerous conditions. That is what a responsible creditor must do. China should show the way."[8] The fate of the Belt and Road no doubt hangs on how the Chinese authorities are able to manage this set of issues, even if their approach is likely to deviate considerably from that advocated by the *Financial Times*. Their instinct is more political than financial, their priority to control the sources of income and be relatively less strict on the dispensations of credit.

As serious as it may become, China's debt threat may be exaggerated by not taking into account the peculiarities of the Chinese economy. As Andrew Nathan explains, just as the US dollar enjoys the "exorbitant privilege" of being accepted everywhere as a bearer of value even though it is not backed by any tangible asset, so too the Chinese yuan—which is not freely convertible—must be accepted by participants in the Chinese economy—on its way to becoming the world's largest—which gives the government the ability to print money at will in order to stimulate economic growth, with limited risk of inflation.

Counter critique

Given the nature of China's economy, both debtors and creditors are mostly government entities, so the government can adjust their debt relationships without precipitating a financial panic.[9]

As the problems with their international investment projects keep growing, China's development banks have decided to intensify their cooperation with overseas financial institutions. China Development Bank is reportedly considering combining its lending efforts with Western financial institutions that require adherence to "international standards"—including open, competitive tenders for project contracts as well as public studies on environmental and social impacts.[10] With open tenders, China's policy banks would be forced to concede loans without the stipulation that Chinese companies must do most of the planned work. Unsurprisingly, as it attempts to mitigate financial risks, China will lose some of the exclusive control over the Belt and Road it has so far enjoyed.

As the Belt and Road initiative gains speed, China is increasingly finding that it cannot provide the required financial resources all on its own. To attempt to fill these needs at home—using Chinese banks—at a time when its economy is slowing down and its banks are saddled with bad loans would expose the financial system to unmanageable risks. Therefore, it is essential for China to gain access to global financial markets to complement its domestic resources. World financial hubs such as Dubai, Singapore, Zurich or even London could play a role.

It is true that China continues to limit access to its financial services market, with cross-border lending and offshore bond issuance facing numerous legal and political limitations. Those familiar with the reasons for China's financial protectionism understand that they are less immediately connected to economic and industrial policy goals than to political imperatives. The determinant of whether a sector of the Chinese economy is open to foreign entities has always been whether state-owned enter-

*BRI – public good + likely m. decen.
since Chi. can't supply needed cap. ✗*

prises are already operating in the area. The Belt and Road is a high political priority for the Chinese government, so this may be the best way to frame wider discussions about financial market access. If the question of opening the Chinese financial services market is a political one, any country seeking to engage it needs to address it as such. There is enormous potential to make progress through dialogue between public and private stakeholders, provided motivations on both sides are properly understood.

It is very likely—perhaps even inevitable—that the Belt and Road will grow more decentralized—less Sinocentric—over time. But this, after all, is not that different from the structure of the existing America-led world order, where the United States insists on being recognized as the state at the apex of the international power hierarchy. Its preeminent role is fully compatible with the preservation of large spheres of autonomy for secondary states, some of which have been admitted to a kind of inner circle where important decisions are made and where their voices are heard. The preferred understanding is that of American leadership rather than domination. Similarly, the Belt and Road may evolve into a complex system where countries occupy different levels in its hierarchy and some may even acquire managing rights in the initiative.

* * *

Chinese commentators are quick to identify the 2008 financial crisis as a turning point, the moment the world realized Western economic and political institutions were far more fragile than everyone thought and the "China solution" acquired new luster, if only by contraposition. But there should be a cautionary note here to the effect that financial crises now decide the fate of nations, their rise and fall, and these critical moments for building the future have a way of arriving unannounced.

Debt has emerged as the main challenge faced by the Belt and Road, but for some commentators it is actually part of the grand scheme. According to this view, China deliberately saddles countries with debt to make them more vulnerable to its influence. If the Hambantota port remains largely idle and the multibillion dollar investment to build it risks being squandered, perhaps this is as intended. One commentator goes so far as to argue that it is better for China if the projects do not do well, because that increases the debt burden for participant countries. Some countries, overwhelmed by their debts loads, are being forced to sell stakes in critical projects or hand over their management to Chinese state-owned firms. "By integrating its foreign, economic, and security policies, China is advancing its goal of fashioning a hegemonic sphere of trade, communication, transportation, and security links. If states are saddled with onerous levels of debt as a result, their financial woes only aid China's neocolonial designs."[11]

The truth is surely somewhere in the middle. In cases like Hambantota port—so unattractive is its geography compared to Colombo—Chinese companies will almost certainly shoulder important losses and having a 99-year lease and a management concession is unlikely to change the outcome. Even if China opens its second overseas naval base there, one might still argue that there were much cheaper ways to reach that outcome. In other cases, debt diplomacy may turn out to be extraordinarily successful as China obtains majority ownership in some of the critical infrastructure of the future world economy. There will be obvious and notable successes—projects that capture our imagination as they get implemented, advances in technology happening faster than expected—helping propel the initiative forward and these will be sufficient to keep the political consensus around it. But the historical analogy always invoked in official statements and documents on the Belt and Road may serve as a warning sign: after all, glorious as they were, the expeditions that the Chinese Admiral Zheng led across the full extension of the Indian Ocean in the fifteenth century were abandoned by later

Ming emperors, opening the way for European control over Asia, starting with the Portuguese at the end of the century. Might a similar fate await the Belt and Road?

Over the second half of 2018, signs of internal discontent with the Belt and Road started to emerge into public view, a development made all the more surprising by the tight control over public expressions of doubt over major policy lines. On August 1, as he voiced his criticism of China's ambitious foreign policy, a retired professor of physics at Shandong University, Sun Wenguang, was seen being taken away by police, while his voice trailed off: "Regular people are poor, let us not throw our money away in Africa. Throwing money around like this does not do any good for our country or our society." The topic of discussion during the hour-long show was China's "throw-money diplomacy." Sun had written an open letter critical of Xi Jinping on the eve of his July trip to Africa and the Middle East. In the letter, he urged Xi to stop spending money overseas on aid, loans and investments, saying the money would be better spent in China.

On 24 July 2018, Xu Zhangrun, a law professor at Tsinghua university, published a lengthy online critique of China's present political and social condition. The essay may seem at times to be part of a Westernizing liberal tradition, but it quickly reveals itself to be anchored in a different political worldview. One theme stands out in this respect: the critique of "excessive international aid." For a developing country with a large population many of whom still live in a pre-modern economy, such behavior is outrageously disproportionate, Xu argues, stressing that average Chinese are most frequently offended by the way the state scatters large sums of money through international aid to little or no benefit. Money earned in China must be spent in China. For Xu, the internationalism of the Belt and Road is no more than a form of vanity politics or flashy showmanship. At this point he appeals directly to the masses with language meant to evoke their ire: "Rural destitution is a widespread and crushing reality; greater support through public policy initiatives is essential. Without major changes, half of China will remain in what is basically a pre-modern economic state. That will mean that the hope to create a modern China will remain unfulfilled, if not half-hearted."[12]

From the outset, the fear that time would wear off the consensus around the initiative encouraged Xi Jinping and his circle of advisors to run greater risks and make the Belt and Road so critical to the Chinese leadership and the Chinese Communist Party that it can no longer be abandoned. Enshrined in the Party Constitution, it stands above criticism. Setbacks will be down-played—they could be financial or affect the life and security of Chinese citizens abroad—and every success magnified. With the elimination of presidential term limits Xi can think and plan on the very long time scale upon which success and failure are in this case to be measured. And that is highly revealing of the best way to answer the question of whether the Belt and Road will succeed. In fact, the initiative is so formless and multidimensional—it is an operating system, not a program or application—that the question as such makes no sense, unless we think in less binary terms. Create a list with all the—properly weighed—goals of the Belt and Road. One can discuss whether 70 or 60 or perhaps 50 per cent of them will be realized, but to use a single measure of success is as misleading as it is impossible to conceptualize.

The second question is how to define success. Where do Chinese authorities want to take their country? What China do they imagine after the Belt and Road and how will the initiative contribute to bring about the transformation? We know that the plans are bold and ambitious. Above all, they are not limited to China, but are explicitly meant to transform the world system as a whole. Many other initiatives have as their goal to bring about changes in China's economy and society. What sets the Belt and

Road apart is its global scope and the awareness that certain elements of China's rise can only take place if the world as a whole adjusts to it.

In November 2012, two weeks after he was elected General Secretary of the Central Committee of the Communist Party of China, Xi Jinping visited "The Road Towards Renewal", an exhibition at the National Museum of China in Beijing. There, in the company of other members of the Politburo, he made a speech celebrating the struggles the country has been through in its history and his hopes for a bright future. It culminated with the sentence: "I firmly believe that the great dream of the renewal of the Chinese nation will come true." The dream is, first of all, one of national renewal or rejuvenation. There can be no doubt that the image of the dream is meant to refer us to the long historical period known by the Chinese as the 'century of humiliation', when the country succumbed to Western control and domination after being defeated militarily in the Opium Wars. This was the fate delivered to China at gunpoint in 1840: either accept "the extinction of the nation and the people," or, like Japan, take the path of complete Westernization. In 1854 the US Navy began to patrol the Yangtze River to protect American interests in the distant Chinese interior, ending these patrols only when forced to do so by Japan in the Second World War.

The historical narrative restarts with the founding of the Chinese Communist Party in 1921, whose centenary approaches, and then 1949, when the "New China was established." At that point, as Chinese leaders are keen to put it, the Chinese people acquired a "pillar" in their pursuit of national liberation. Their psychological attitude changed "from passivity to agency" and they started to grasp their national fate in their own hands. The last Party Congress in 2017 spoke in this context of a "spirit of struggle." If the Chinese people want to free themselves from the Western model which has kept the whole world in subjugation, then it needs to engage in uncompromising struggle. History looks kindly on those with resolve, with drive and ambition and courage, but it will not wait for those who are hesitant. China is now at the decisive moment when it must make that choice.

In a meeting behind closed doors with members of the Central Military Commission in February 2017—at the end of the five-year term initiated at the National Museum exhibition—Xi criticized Western democracy, saying many Western countries promote "democratic expansion" and see themselves as the "world savior," while their institutions create not only societal divisions, but also infighting among parties and endless political scandals. Many leaders of developing countries are thus doubtful about the political system of the West, and expressed hope to learn about how China has developed. "We are now facing a historic opportunity that happens only once in a thousand years," he concluded. "If we handle it well, we will prosper. But if we screw it up, there will be problems, big problems."[13]

This is the scope of China's current ambition. The Belt and Road will succeed to the extent that it helps propel China's rise to its last stage, its denouement or, so to speak, the announced terminus of its prophetic history.

* * *

There are a number of possible scenarios for China's future place in the world system. In the first, the country would become a prosperous and successful economy, at the same time converging to a Western political and social model. Like West Germany and Japan in the past, it would not attempt to dislodge American power from the center of the world system, perhaps out of a belief that without that cornerstone the system itself cannot survive, or perhaps because such a revolution in world affairs, as almost always in the past, could only happen after a war for hegemony which nuclear weapons have rendered impossible. One could also argue that American power is elusive and based on civil society networks. It tends to be most effective when appealing directly to individuals rather than to the states whose citizens they are, and if this is the case only global public opinion rather than the Chinese state can hope to overthrow it. As Oliver Stuenkel writes in a recent book, it is possible to argue that, by creating a parallel structure of institutions, China is not setting out to destroy the Western-led order. Its initiatives in the realms of finance, currency, infrastructure, trade and security—most of them now subsumed under the Belt and Road—are meant to provide China with alternatives, to reduce its dependency on the existing order and limit risks, without thereby reducing its support for the current order. Indeed, he thinks that the West should support these efforts: "Even though Beijing will be careful to design new institutions to its advantage, they will still force China to agree to a specific set of governance rules, which must make its behavior far more predictable than it is in the context of bilateral engagements. All these institutions will deepen China's integration into the global economy, possibly reducing the risk for conflict, and lifting all boats."[14]

The second scenario is also one of convergence, but it introduces a critical difference. Although committed to the general principles of the liberal world system, and while converging to some variety of Western politics, China would strive to and perhaps even succeed in replacing the United States as the center of political and economic power. This is a scenario that seems to fit reasonably well with the main goals behind the Belt and Road. The initiative seems to share some of the organizing principles of the global order as it exists at present—connectivity, openness and interdependence—while advancing Chinese economic and political interests. The scenario is also agreeable to those who see in the Trump presidency a retreat from global leadership, opening the way for China to take over from the United States as the guardian of a global order from which it has undoubtedly benefited much.

In this scenario, the Belt and Road would play a critical role. It would provide China with increased leverage, allowing it to exert pressure on the United States so that the existing international system could be reformed in a way that allowed China to have a degree of influence commensurate with its economic clout. But it would not be a tool to replace it with a new system since the existing one, generally speaking, still works quite well for China.[15] When President Xi spoke in Davos in early 2017 he seemed to be saying just that, reassuring the audience that China was not about to embrace radical changes to the existing order—Davos is not the place to do that—while staking a claim to increase its power and influence. He Yafei, a former Chinese vice foreign minister, wrote in 2017 that "new emerging economies and developing countries represented by China strongly support globalization, while some Western countries including the US, the initiators and leaders of globalization, have reversed their positions."[16]

Ultimately, the existing global order may prove more resilient than the sinews of American power supporting it. Even if China surpasses the United States, it is not clear that it will be able to create something new. "Even if China surpasses the United States in power capabilities, it is not clear that it will be able to overturn the existing international order. This is true not only because the United States is just one of many stake holders in the existing order. China will need to offer the world a vision of international order that is legitimate and functional. As China becomes more powerful, it will certainly seek greater authority and rights within the existing order—and the existing order is configured in a way that can allow this to happen. But can it preside over an epochal transformation of the liberal international order into something radically new? Not likely."[17]

THE WORLD AFTER THE BELT AND ROAD

America's China strategy for the past three decades—perhaps even longer—seems to have been articulated by reference to my first scenario above, at most countenancing very limited elements from the second. During the second Bush administration Robert Zoellick explained that the United States wanted China to become a "responsible stakeholder" in the existing international system. What this would mean was left purposefully ambiguous, but its conservative element was clear enough: China was supposed to find a place within the international system without forcing too many changes upon its structure. If Japan had grown into the second largest economy in the world without disturbing the status quo—while reinforcing it as a matter of fact—the same could perhaps be expected of China. To ease things, Washington might be willing to make a number of concessions, granting Beijing a level of influence over global rules and institutions that its more direct allies were never able to attain. To this day officials in Beijing will quote Zoellick when defending the Belt and Road: Western countries want us to be a responsible stakeholder and contribute more to the provision of global public goods, that is what we intend to do with our broad initiative.

My third scenario poses the possibility of a normative clash between two visions of the world order. The reader will likely be already inclined to recognize its appeal and implications. The starting point: China is not converging with a Western political model. None of the private or public statements emanating from Beijing allow us to think otherwise. The image of the global order promoted by the Belt and Road differs in dramatic ways from the image of a liberal global order as it exists today and thus its success will not only mean that a different actor will move to the center of global power but also that that the system itself will be differently organized and the values it embodies will form a new constellation. In June 2018 Yao Yunzhu, a retired major-general of the Chinese People's Liberation Army, said the international order needed to be rewritten after failing to heed China's growth. She cited the South China Sea as an example where the rules needed to be rewritten in response to territorial disputes and criticism that China has been constructing islands and militarizing them by building runways and missile systems. In January 2018 Joe Kaeser, CEO of German industrial giant Siemens, had made the same point about a Chinese world order with a pithy sentence: "China's Belt and Road will be the new World Trade Organization—whether we like it or not."[18]

Once great power competition invades the realm of fundamental values, everything changes. Suddenly initiatives such as the Belt and Road cease to be regarded as normal acts of diplomacy or exercises in soft power. While not hard in the sense of military force, nor can they be considered soft. They represent a direct challenge, an attack on the foundations of Western liberal societies by the mere fact of propagating a different and opposing vision and evoking the sense of a final clash for supremacy or even survival. Some have therefore tried to develop a new concept of "sharp power," capturing the clash between different regimes or visions of society.[19]

On a wide range of issues from the Internet to human rights and sovereignty claims in the South China Sea or global trade, China is putting forth a clear challenge to the existing liberal order. It is one openly advocated by Chinese officials and intellectuals, although they obviously regard these differences not as failures to live up to Western values but as the affirmation of a different system carrying different values or, perhaps more aptly, different virtues: principles of amity, sincerity, mutual benefit and inclusiveness furthering a community of shared destiny.

The Belt and Road would provide an obvious conduit to export important elements of China's political regime. In Ethiopia, for example, ZTE Corporation has already sold technology and provided training to monitor mobile phones and Internet activity and in Kenya Huawei is partnering with the government to con-struct "safe cities" that leverage thousands of surveillance cameras feeding data into a public security cloud. And when it comes to the global debate on human rights and democracy, it hardly needs to be stressed that countries beholden to China's financial largesse will be more likely to side with it.[20]

Seen from Beijing, the new world order would be replacing a model whose failures have become all too obvious. State Councilor Yang Jiechi observed in November 2017 that it had become "increasingly difficult for Western governance concepts, systems, and models to keep up with the new international situation." Western-led global governance, he argued, had "malfunctioned," and the accumulation of "various ills" showed the system had reached a point "beyond redemption."[21] Humanity is facing huge natural, technological, economic, social, and security challenges. Solutions to these problems will require us to pool resources, plans, and development mechanisms across the world, but existing models seem increasingly unable to deliver them. Collective decisions to fight climate change are weak and insufficient. Many countries have entered long periods of state failure or civil wars and the international community seems closer to giving up on peace efforts altogether than to brokering a negotiated solution. As a result, terrorism has become an existential threat to many societies and the number of refugees worldwide keeps growing. Western efforts arguably made things worse, as in the case of recent military interventions in the Middle East. Global tensions are as high as in the worst moments of the Cold War, with the difference that we now lack an adequate framework to address and minimize them.

Chinese authorities thus have some ground to argue that the world as a whole is facing a dire governance crisis, that the West has run out of ideas and therefore that it is perhaps time for others to take up the task. "Western countries have frequently been limited by their own theories of international cooperation, either believing it requires the presence of a hegemon to be viable, or that it can only take place under the auspices of Western democratic models. The model of international cooperation that China advances, meanwhile, is naturally non-hegemonic and open to a diversity of political systems."[22] Following the 19th Party Congress, Foreign Minister Wang Yi elaborated on the CPC's approach to global leadership, stating that "China will actively explore a way of resolving hotspot issues with Chinese characteristics and play a bigger and more constructive role in upholding world stability." This implies that the country will become proactive in regions in crisis, perhaps intensifying its efforts there due to the growing number of Chinese workers and investments abroad. In Afghanistan, Beijing seems to have adopted a transactional, flexible approach—implying an alternative to the Western development model. Beijing may provide less aid to Afghanistan than Western countries, but its aid is delivered quickly and without preconditions. "Resolving hotspot issues with Chinese characteristics" also indicates that "China wants to engage with different stakeholders in hotspot regions as compared to countries in the West that differentiate between democracies and dictators."[23] During the drafting of the UN Sustainable Development Goals, which set development priorities for the UN's 193 member states, China was among those opposing a goal that called for "freedom of media, association, and speech." Chinese resistance helped to ensure that the goals adopted in September 2015 featured much vaguer language and entirely missed media independence or the freedoms of speech and association.

The Belt and Road represents a major change in developmental philosophy, an alternative development model, a complete break with the ideas now dominant in western-led institutions such as the International Monetary Fund and the World Bank,

where development is no longer seen as bricks-and-mortar building of factories and bridges, but as institution-building and
policy change. As Branko Milanovic puts it, the Belt and Road
proposes an activist view of development: "you need roads for
farmers to bring their goods, you need fast railroads, bridges to
cross the rivers, tunnels to link communities living at different
ends of a mountain." And it will not deal in any of the moralizing
prescriptions about institutions, rule of law, transparency, local
empowerment and so on that now dominate Western views on
development. "While in some quarters, this may be thought as a
defect," Milanovic concludes, "in others, it may be considered a
plus: it will clearly distinguish between mutual economic self-
interest and other political or cultural domains."[24]

The number one question is whether China will succeed in
reshaping the global order or, alternatively, whether that order
might fracture into two opposing and irreconcilable visions, the
defining mark of the fourth scenario in my classification.
Remarkably, the Belt and Road could prove a winning strategy
in that scenario as well, thus illustrating what a flexible tool it
can be. As trade tensions between China and the US intensified
in June 2018, officials in Beijing argued that China should press
ahead with the initiative as a way to secure export markets and
diversify from its excessive reliance on the American market.
Shoring up relations with important customers along the Belt
and Road was seen as a way to preempt US attempts to turn
them against China in the case of a protracted economic conflict
between the two countries. In July 2018 China's State Council
issued a revealing set of import guidelines as trade tensions esca-
lated with the US. Companies should "look to Belt and Road
countries as a new source of imports, strengthen strategic cooperation, and increase imports of high-quality products that meet
the needs of upgraded domestic consumption in order to expand
the scale of trade."[25] From January to May, China imported

1.1 trillion yuan in goods from countries involved in the Belt and Road Initiative, an increase of 15.1% year-on-year, and 3.4% points higher than the overall growth rate of imports. Instead of integrating into the existing world order, China could be creating a separate economic bloc, with different dominant companies and technologies, and governed by rules, institutions, and trade patterns dictated by Beijing.[26]

A balance between China and the United States may take place within the framework of common values and principles or it may be organized around fundamental differences on the question of the world order. Increasingly, it seems that Chinese leaders regard the ability to break with the liberal world order as a measure of their success and the Belt and Road as the main tool to bring about an alternative vision.

Convergence was a powerful idea, perhaps the most powerful foreign policy idea of the last three decades. As Thomas Wright puts it, everyone or almost everyone believed that as countries embraced globalization their political systems would become more liberal and democratic. "Citizens of other nations believed it, too, including many Russians, Chinese, Indians, and Brazilians. It mattered not whether you were on the left or the right; almost everyone bought into the basic notion of convergence, even if they were unfamiliar with the term."[27] Very few believe it today, at least when it comes to China. In the West, the recent decision to abolish presidential term limits, opening the way for Xi Jinping to rule for life, made it clear that China is treading its own path. Whatever liberal currents there have been in the past, they have been marginalized in the power struggle within China.

Once we get rid of what Wright calls the "myth of convergence," the stakes become much higher. America and China are separated not only by divergent interests, some of which could conceivably be reconciled, but by incompatible visions for the future of Asia and the world. China's current rulers may not be trying actively to spread their own unique blend of repressive politics and a mixed economy, but as they have become richer and stronger they have begun to act in ways that inspire and strengthen friendly regimes, while potentially weakening the institutions of young and developing democracies.[28] *Adam Freedberg Survival*

* * *

The strategic issue today is which paradigm of international relations will ultimately prevail. On the one hand, we see a return to a vision of global politics as marked by a renewed competition for spheres of influence. This is the paradigm of national interests and its defining characteristic is the absence of common or overlapping perspectives. On the other hand, however much their influence has been attenuated, it is still the case that common institutions and cooperative relations dominate most relations between states. Globalization has not retreated, interdependence has intensified and states must still engage in multiple cooperative endeavors. From this perspective, China is certainly right to emphasize ideas of interdependence and the United States and Europe will regret not offering rival initiatives that can promote the same goals. The struggle to find common perspectives and ways to manage common challenges and problems continues unabated. It is perhaps less formalized, more chaotic and, as a result, its outcomes have become correspondingly uncertain or even unpredictable.

The belief in universal values is a fair description of how many in the West see world politics, but this vision is increasingly difficult to sustain. In the case of Russia, the rejection of Western values is complete and definitive. In a first stage, Russian leaders still spoke approvingly of adopting modern European norms and standards, even if this was always combined with the assertion that a "common European home" would be multipolar and could not simply absorb Russia into existing structures. After the Ukraine crisis, the break went much deeper and the Kremlin has even flirted with the notion that Russia is now much more interested in its relations with China than in its old and halting movement towards Europe. As for the question of whether China and Russia may be somehow ordained to come into conflict—a question I am repeatedly asked—it is critical to keep in mind that they both see their priority as the creation of a new, multipolar world order. Such an order is, by definition, one where different actors struggle to preserve and extend their spheres of influence, something about which China and Russia might well have disagreements—but for the next two decades they will be focused on the former question of what kind of world order will prevail.

In China the European Union and the United States face an even greater challenge. While Russian revisionism may still be shrugged off as incapable of durable consequences for the global order—Russia might after all become an increasingly marginal state, incapable of solving its modernization problems—China now offers an alternative model with an increasingly global appeal. In the past, the belief that China would ultimately follow the adoption of a capitalist market economy with the corresponding conversion to liberal democracy helped define Western foreign policy. That particular illusion has been abandoned. We realize much better now that even countries on the same modernization path may end up in very different places. On the one hand, the very idea of a modern society now appears to us as far more capacious than hitherto. Its basic elements—abstract social relations and the widespread use of technology—are compatible with a myriad of different ways of life. Even the path taken by Western societies could easily reveal junctures where different alternatives might have been pursued.

Washington's strategy of drawing China in—it may sound odd, but for a long time China's isolation and poverty rather than Chinese influence were seen as a major threat to global stability—and helping it along a trajectory of economic growth in the hope that a growing middle class would in time push for democratic reforms, turned out to be a failure. Above all, it was a failure of imagination, revealing of a deep incapacity to understand the world on its own terms and to step out of rigid ideological models. Nothing in the history of Western political and economic models allows us to believe that current solutions were preordained, and if they were not preordained for us they certainly are not inevitable for Chinese society. But it was also a failure of practical politics. China was by far the greatest beneficiary of global trade and economic arrangements over the past three decades. A study by the MIT economist David Autor and colleagues calculated that Chinese competition cost the US some 2.4 million jobs between 1999 and 2011, battering factory towns that made labor-intensive goods.[29] Trying to convince Congress to vote in favor of China's accession to the World Trade Organization, President Bill Clinton had argued in the spring of 2000 that China was not simply "agreeing to import more of our products, it is agreeing to import one of democracy's most cherished values, economic freedom," and realizing the vision of "a world full of free markets, free elections and free peoples working together." As far as predictions go, this turned out to be spectacularly wrong. As James Mann argued in his *The China Fantasy*, American policymakers found in the myth of convergence a powerful anesthetic and tranquilizer, allowing them to defend the status quo on the grounds that China's exposure to the benefits of globalization would lead the country to embrace democratic institutions and support the American-led world order. Instead, Mann predicted, China would remain an authoritarian country, and its success would encourage other authoritarian regimes to resist pressures to change.[30]

Western decision-makers were willing to agree to an informal bargain where China would receive Western technology under the assumption that it would be just as open to Western political and economic ideas. The second half of the bargain never materialized. The United States and the European Union now find themselves in the position of having to develop a new China strategy practically overnight, as they try to catch up with the Belt and Road rollercoaster.

On the other hand, the choices made in the West—Western values but also technical solutions only loosely related to those values—have lost their immediacy and appeal. The 2008 financial crisis, the rise of populism, the growing inability to deal with the consequences of a diminished global status—all these moments have awakened Western self-doubt where before only missionary zeal was manifest.

Chinese elites—and broader tendencies in Chinese public opinion tend to follow them—implicitly believe that to move closer to Western values or to attempt to imitate the West in different areas would be tantamount to abdicating China's edge, opting to compete on territory defined by the West and therefore on terms clearly tilted in its favor. As a recent report puts it, if in the eighteenth century a Chinese emperor famously explained to a British embassy that he had no need for Western goods, the view in China today is that the country has no need for Western culture, ideas and values.[31]

Two issues stand out and will have critical consequences for relations between China and the West. First, on the question of reciprocity, the West now recognizes that China is unlikely to accept at home those norms of economic openness and market governance from which it benefits when its companies operate in the American and European markets. The difficulty here is that full reciprocity can only be established if the West renounces all pretense to the universality of its own values and starts to exclude China from the purview of a system of norms once intended for all. Closing the borders to Chinese investment or applying new tariffs and regulatory barriers to Chinese exports on the grounds that China does the same may serve different purposes: it could be an attempt to influence China to change its ways or, on the contrary, a measure meant to protect Western markets from Chinese intrusion. In practice we are likely to end up with some combination of these two goals. A multipolar world system would be based on different spheres of influence, as different actors pursue independent paths, even if they are also able—in limited areas—to influence and shape each other's system of norms.

The second major issue is directly related to security and the role of international law. As China pushes its own national interest in such conflict areas as the South China Sea and its disputed border areas with India, the West—in this case the European Union more than the United States—has an important stake in defending the status of international law and rules-based methods for conflict resolution, but the challenge in this case is that those positions will increasingly be impossible to defend if the European Union continues lagging behind China and the United States in hard power. Conversely, if Europeans come to a common understanding that their values now need to be supported with better tools of power projection, might that conclusion not raise doubts about whether the EU is sacrificing its own values in response to a new world of cut-throat competition?

The National Security Strategy approved by President Trump in December 2017 radically breaks with the traditional strategy of convergence: "The United States helped expand the liberal economic trading system to countries that did not share our values, in the hopes that these states would liberalize their economic and political practices and provide commensurate benefits to the United States. Experience shows that these countries distorted and undermined key economic institutions without undertaking significant reform of their economies or politics. They espouse free trade rhetoric and exploit its benefits, but only adhere selec-

179

tively to the rules and agreements."[32] The document advocates that the United States distinguish between those countries that adhere to the same values and those that do not. With like-minded states competition should happen in the "economic domain," but with other states competition is taken to the political level, where it should be conducted through "enforcement measures." Every year—the document argues—countries such as China steal intellectual property valued at hundreds of billion of dollars, an economic and security risk to which the United States will respond with counterintelligence and law enforcement activities to curtail intellectual property theft by all sources, while exploring new legal and regulatory mechanisms to prevent and prosecute violations. This is a world where competition, not cooperation is the predominant reality. Values are less the common perspective of all nations than a specific way of life targeted by one's enemies and adversaries. They are antithetical. As the strategy puts it in a crucial passage, "China and Russia want to shape a world antithetical to U.S. values and interests."[33]

We are thus at a critical juncture when the language of values may enter a period of crisis. Antithetical values are a difficult concept to defend. It may be seen as internally contradictory: if each state actor defends its own set of values, it can no longer endow them with universal significance. Valid only for the agent asserting them, they may become too dependent on the logic of state power and conflict. In order to rebuild the concept of values on a new plane, the effort to bridge differences and find common ground will have to begin anew. At the current moment, that effort still seems to lie far in the future.

But west swears not'l

* * *

What changed in the last two or three years is that China is no longer satisfied with waging an ideological war at home—staving off Western challenges to party rule—but wants to take that war to the world stage. It can no longer be said that the Chinese are indifferent to how other peoples govern themselves. In his opening speech to the Communist Party's 19th Congress in October 2017, Xi Jinping spoke frankly about posing an ideological challenge to Western liberal democracy. China is "blazing a new trail for other developing countries to achieve modernization," providing "a new option for other countries and nations who want to speed up their development".

The difficulty is not one of devising the contours of a specific Chinese model, but the sense that such a model would remain of limited validity or that only Western values can claim to be genuinely universal. Many in Russia, the Islamic world and elsewhere have tried to question that universality, but usually they do so by arguing that no political value can aspire to be universal. That may have been the line in Beijing as well, but the time now is to go on the offensive. Waiting for us in the near future, as the writer Jinghan Zeng argues, is a China that is likely to become the largest world economy, offering a distinct growth model backed up by military power, and actively exporting its ideological beliefs. At the 19th Party Congress, Xi Jinping set "the mid-21st century" as the deadline to fulfill those promises.[34]

The Belt and Road calls for universal values of a new kind and Chinese authors have taken that task to heart. On the one hand, one can easily identify fractures within the Western political tradition. Roads not taken, contemporary contradictions, excesses and contagions of different kinds. Many of the flaws in that tradition have been explored in detail by Western authors. Their work stands ready to be used. On the other hand, traditional alternatives may be reconfigured and made to serve new purposes in a modern society. Chinese culture places wholeness and synthesis above individuality, traits that seem able to survive even as China becomes a fully modern society.

Be that as it may, China has a number of indisputable achievements to show for itself in recent decades: many hundreds of millions of people were pulled out of poverty—or better put, pulled themselves out of poverty—while Chinese society modernized quickly, developing new technology and building infrastructure that now seems to overshadow that of the West. It must be possible to theorize these achievements, discover what explains them, the political and social traits behind China's rise, and then these could plausibly be applied elsewhere.

Popular Chinese authors such as Zhang Weiwei argue that the Western model has failed by not being able to provide for a genuine separation of powers. In a modern state, he writes, at least three powers are permanently interacting with each other, thus shaping the trajectory and the fate of that country: political, social and financial. Indeed, a modern political system of good governance should be able to guarantee that there be an equilibrium of the political, social and capital powers to act in favor of the interests of the majority. In the case of the United States, predominance of financial power over political and social powers have sapped the strength of system and perhaps even poisoned the American dream.

What then explains China's success, what are the political values underpinning its dramatic rise over the past three decades? Zhang seems to think the fundamental value is the spirit of "seeking truth from facts," which he is convinced has been abandoned by Western societies. There are so many ideological taboos in Western political and social life and to be politically correct has become far more important than to be able to "grasp reality." Is this because democracy and the knowledge of reality have come into contradiction, because ideas that are acceptable to all have become more important that true ideas? Zhang does not spell it out, but he believes that only the ability to grasp reality can provide a solid basis for politics. In its absence the clash of different sources of power and opposing social groups will lead to chaos and disorder. Different interest groups will battle for power, each using every political and legal tool to prevent reforms and protect its privileges.

In a spectacular reversal of our traditional assumptions, Western societies appear captured by the status quo, unable to embrace change and in mortal danger of losing their dynamism. China, by contrast, represents social and economic improvement or, as Zhang calls it, good governance. The West wants to prevent certain outcomes—democracy and rights are meant to prevent the illegitimate use of power—while China wants to bring about positive outcomes. Churchill's famous dictum that democracy is the worst form of government except for all those other forms that have been tried may be appealing in the Western cultural context. For Zhang, the Chinese path is not to avoid the worst but to strive for the best.[35] In the old quarrel between philosophy and democracy, China seems to be siding with philosophy.

In an essay published in the Guangzhou journal *Open Times* in January 2018, the Peking University constitutional lawyer Jiang Shigong tries to show why Xi Jinping's thought provides the right framework for a new historical period when China will occupy the center of the world system. 'Standing up', 'getting rich', and 'becoming powerful' are ways to divide the histories of the Party and the Republic, referring respectively to the Mao Zedong era, the Deng Xiaoping era, and the Xi Jinping era that we are currently entering. History does not unfold naturally; it is created by "leaders leading people." Western thought may attempt to obscure this truth, in which case it is Western thought that must be overcome. As Jiang puts it, the construction of China's rule of law gradually fell into the erroneous zone of Western concepts in the process of studying the Western rule of law, and consciously or not, the notions of 'rule of law' and 'rule of man' came to be seen as antagonistic. "We overly fetishized legal dogma and institutional reforms and came to understand the rule of law simplistically as a machine in which rules functioned automatically, overlooking the fact that if we want to use 'good laws' to carry out 'good governance' then we need good social culture and moral values to systematically support the effective functioning of legal institutions and regulations."

Faced with the Western ban on truly creative human action and decisions, China sees itself as embracing the openness of history and the inception of a new age. The Belt and Road takes its significance from the search for the future of human civilization. Whether Chinese civilization will make new contributions to all of mankind remains of course to be seen—the story of the century is only now beginning—but its efforts take place in the realm of those world-changing or world-shaping endeavors providing humanity with a future vision of an ideal life, endeavors the West was once capable of but whose creative springs now reside elsewhere. This means not only the end to the global political landscape of Western civilization's domination since the age of great discoveries, but also breaking the global dominance of Western civilization in the past half a millennium in the cultural sense, and hence ushering in a new era in human progress.[36]

Zhang Weiwei and Jiang Shigong may be right or wrong on these points of doctrine. That in the end is not the question. What their arguments show is that, far from suffering from a dearth of alternatives, we have too many universal values to choose from and they are evidently not compatible or even fully commensurable between them.

When discussing world politics today, we often revert to one of two models. The first, popularized by Francis Fukuyama, sees the whole world converging to a European or Western political framework, after which no further historical development is possible. Every country or region is measured by the time it will still take to reach this final destination, but all doubts and debates about where we are heading have been fundamentally resolved. The other model, defended by Samuel Huntington, is skeptical of such irreversible movement. The world it depicts is that of a clash between different civilizations having little or nothing in common, particularly since Western political culture will remain geographically limited. But there is a third way, which I tried to develop in my book *The Dawn of Eurasia.* I agree with Fukuyama that the whole world is on the path to modern society, but there are numerous paths and, naturally, different visions of what a modern society looks like.

Everyone is modern now, but there are different models of modern society. From this fact the essential terms of the new world order follow more or less directly. The hard distinction between modern and traditional has broken down, giving way to a deeply integrated world, but its most distinctive trait is the incessant competition between different ideas of how worldwide networks should be organized.

* * *

Let us recapitulate our four scenarios. In the first, China is gradually integrated into the liberal world order. Its political model converges with that of Western liberal democracies, even as it continues to show some distinctive traits. Its economy grows, reaching parity with the United States and approaching Western standards of living. The two countries effectively rule the world economy together, but on other dimensions of global power—political, military, cultural—China does not attempt to overturn American hegemony.

In the second scenario, China replaces the United States as the center of global power, but everything else remains more or less the same. The Chinese political and economic model converges with Western patterns—but less drastically than in the first scenario—and, more importantly, the liberal world order survives unscathed: multilateral institutions, open trade, international cooperation on common challenges and even some form of individual and community rights.

The third scenario is one where China takes over from the Unites States as the center of global power with the result that the very structure and values of the world system are rethought and reconfigured. The liberal world order is replaced with a Chinese order, Western values give way to Chinese values and the pace of historical development is increasingly dictated from Beijing.

In the fourth scenario two visions of the world order are forced to coexist: China and the United States need to reach some kind of balance, either through a division of the world into two distinct spheres of influence or as some combination or compound where integration goes together with conflict and rivalry.

The year is 2049, one hundred years after the founding of the People's Republic. Following its century of national humiliation, China stood up, became rich, and ultimately grew more and more powerful. The Belt and Road is complete. That does not mean it will stop or disappear. It is concluded in the same way a bridge or a road is built. Its development is finished and it is ready to start working or operating at full power. Some of the infrastructure projects are truly stunning and now stand as the highest example of what human ingenuity can achieve in its drive to master natural forces. A bridge crossing the Caspian Sea—200 km from Azerbaijan to Turkmenistan—has made road transport between Europe and China fast and easy, changing old mental maps separating continents. The Kra Isthmus Canal in Thailand has done the same for the Indian and Pacific Oceans. No longer do we think of them as two separate oceans. Sea transportation is now entirely conducted by autonomous seafaring freighters. Shipyards based in southern China have dominated the "ghost ship" market ever since the first model, the *Somersault Cloud*, named after the magical cloud that transports the Monkey King in the classic Chinese saga *Journey to the West*. In Africa a high-speed railway connects the two coasts, traversing Djibouti, Ethiopia, South Sudan, Central African Republic and Cameroon in under twenty hours. Trade between Africa, Asia and South America increasingly uses this route.

In the meantime, the third segment of the initiative, announced in its second decade, is progressing apace. Self-driving vehicles on land, sea and air and trillions of connected devices worldwide are already empowered by a Belt, Road and Space fleet of China-centered satellites. China now regularly flies reusable space planes and has them carry taikonauts and freight into space. More dramatically, a nuclear-powered spacecraft has been used for the first manned Chinese Martian mission. Chinese companies regularly engage in deep-space economic activity, like building orbit solar power plants, and mining asteroids and the moon. As the head of the Chinese lunar exploration program, Ye Peijian, remarked, "the universe is an ocean, the moon is the Diaoyu Islands, Mars is Huangyan Island. If we don't go there now even though we're capable of doing so, then we will be blamed by our descendants. If others go there, then they will take over, and you won't be able to go even if you want to." Satellites equipped with new quantum sensor technologies are able to identify and track targets that were once invisible from space, such as stealth bombers taking off at night. Ghost imaging satellites have two cameras, one aiming at the targeted area of interest with a bucket-like, single-pixel sensor while the other camera measures variations in a wider field of light across the environment. Nothing can hide from them.

On earth, new cities have grown in once desolate or forbidden landscapes. They have already gone through many stages of transformation: logistics hubs ravaged by crime and corruption to booming immigration metropoles attracting vast influxes of migrants and refugees spurned by the United States and the European Union and finally economic powerhouses of low regulation where successive technological revolutions take no more than a few years. Many successful entrepreneurs have moved to new cities in Central Asia in order to be equally close to China and Europe. Many of the new cities have sizable Chinese populations. These Chinese expats are the entrepreneurs and investment bankers, the trend setters and technology prophets. In many countries in Central Asia, Southeast Asia and Africa, Mandarin has already replaced English as the international lingua franca.

Global Energy Interconnection, a Belt and Road project, has created an intercontinental energy grid, so as to optimize large-scale allocation of clean energy, across wide areas and with high efficiency setting up global regulation and control systems, so that the intercontinental and transnational electricity trade volume accounts for almost half of global electricity consumption. By 2030, the interconnections of Africa-Europe, Asia-Europe and Asia-Africa were formed; by 2040, the interconnections of North America-South America, Oceania-Asia and Asia-North America; by 2049, the interconnection of Europe-North America, and the whole planet relies on a few clean energy bases, including those in the Arctic, the wind power base, and the Equator, the solar power base.

Is this still a recognizable world? Is it still the world we live in today, only more balanced and more divided between different economic poles in Europe, Asia and America? Is it the world of globalization as we have come to know it? In her own "speculative leap into Eurasia's future," Nadège Rolland describes a world where people do not "google," have a Facebook or Twitter account, or watch the news on CNN or the BBC. Instead, they "baidu," use Weibo for their social connections, and watch China Global Television Network. Children do not play "cowboys and Indians" but mimic the exploits of the Monkey King, one of their favorite heroes from the *Journey to the West* tale. Eurasian youths seek acceptance to the highly regarded universities of Beijing, Xian, Urumqi, and Kunming, whose degrees are recognized across the region. These schools offer substantial scholarships to the best and most promising students of the region and give a guarantee of employment in the local branches of Chinese state-owned enterprises.[37] The description is of course inspired by the existing world order and tries to project a future where China has replaced the United States, but the essential shape of things—institutions, values, and relations—remains largely unmodified. The differences are limited to what China lacks by contrast to the current ruler of the system—Rolland mentions freedom of speech and individual rights—as if a few items of furniture have been lost during the house move and spring cleaning.

Similarly, Jonathan Holslag imagines a future Asian order replicating more or less perfectly the European order we know from the last few decades, with China occupying the core, as Germany and France do in Europe. The area from Shanghai to Chengdu and from Shenyang to Kunming would have turned into a densely developed zone, saturated with middle classes, and boasting advanced industries, internationally renowned brands, and quality services. Fast trains and airlines would channel millions of tourists to quiet or quaint places, to Tibet, emerging as the Chinese Pyrenees, to the Northeast, the future Chinese Alps, to Xinjiang, the new Andalusia, and to the southern beaches, China's Club Med. China's new multinationals would have tied all other Asian countries to the motherland by means of roads, railways, pipelines and financial flows. Japan's fate would be comparable to a depopulating version of the United Kingdom, quietly musing on its glorious past. Southeast Asia, China's Italy, would be vibrant and enthralling, yet heavily penetrated by Chinese companies, banks, and high-livers. The stretch from Bangladesh to Kazakhstan could well be China's Northern Africa and Middle East...[38]

This is unlikely. The kind of transformation we are speculating about here would change everything. The system itself would be differently organized and the goals and values inspiring it would be radically different. The new world would not be one where one piece on the chessboard will be replaced, not even one where the pieces will have been reorganized. It will be a world built anew by very different people and according to very different ideas. David Rennie, Beijing bureau chief for *The Economist*, gets somewhat closer to the truth in his forecasting exercise, projected to 2024. Like Rolland, Rennie starts by imagining a dystopian negation of the West. China's intelligence services, working with the country's technology firms, have turned millions of cars in America, Europe and Asia into remote spying devices, letting Beijing track vehicles in real time and identify passengers with facial-recognition technology. A new international organization, the Global Infrastructure Center, decides which schemes are eligible for billions of dollars in Chinese loans and grants, and picks foreign firms as partners using opaque rules devised by Communist Party planners. But Rennie goes on to describe how the new Chinese-led global economic order is based on fundamentally different ideas and principles. New international courts have been created and they draw no distinction between nations with state-directed and market economies. Its judges take a benign view of subsidies that claim to support national development and believe that sovereign governments, rather than individual businesses, should have the final say in patent disputes. "Rarely mounting direct challenges, China has instead tested, probed and introduced ambiguities into every aspect of global governance. Established powers have not so much acquiesced as proved too weary to resist."[39]

There is another respect in which the Belt and Road as dystopian scenario fails to convince: the way it is predicated on the supposition of a wholesale collapse of the Western political order. The way in which Rolland, for example, defines the future Chinese order as a negation of the West seems to refer us to a previous moment—which she coyly refrains from mentioning—when the two alternatives fought for supremacy, or then a previous moment when the West, consumed by internal conflict and disorder, collapsed on its own. Now, as I argued in *The Dawn of Eurasia*, such a scenario seems unlikely at present and, what is more, seems bound to remain unlikely. This chapter and the preceding one sought to explain why this is the case: one cannot extrapolate from China's extraordinary rise over the past four decades to the shape of future events and developments. On the one hand, the challenges China faces now are fundamentally different in nature—political more than economic, with security concerns raising their ugly head. On the other, that very rise or expansion creates new variables—reactions, responses, changes of attitude, as other countries increasingly regard China as a threat or, at the very least, a competitor.

Moreover, our current historical juncture differs from others in the crucial sense that China's rise does not depend on a technological breakthrough which will remain inaccessible to the West. This is the point where parallels with the corresponding moment in the eighteenth and nineteenth centuries—when the West rose to global preeminence—must necessarily stop. The new world order towards which we are moving is not one where there is a clear centre, but rather one distinguished by the search for balance between different poles. So when we describe a new Chinese world order we have to keep in mind that there will be other shareholders, other shapers, other balancers. In some places it may exist in a pure form; in others there will be some precarious balance or combination; and in still others its influence may well be minimal. The West will diminish in reach and influence, but thirty years from now it will continue to offer a powerful alternative to the Belt and Road, even if it may also be expected to evolve in response to the Chinese challenge. The problem for us is to determine the core of the new Chinese world picture and identify the main traits which—unremittingly—it will come to impress upon the whole.

Different political concepts will share the same space, much as if the age of globalization had merged with an older age of different ethical or religious views. The new world order shares with the last decade of the previous century the belief in the inevitability of interdependency and connectivity, but it combines it with the recognition of division and conflict. We have entered the second age of globalization, where borders become increasingly diffuse but cultural and civilizational differences do not, giving rise to a permanently unstable compound of heterogeneous elements. That is why I prefer to speak of the world after the Belt and Road rather than the Belt and Road world. The Belt and Road may never become universal—just as the West never became universal—but in some areas it will rule unimpeded and different shades of influence will be felt everywhere.

As we have seen in preceding chapters, the new Chinese Tianxia may remind us of the American-led order in some important respects—a network of economic relations used to exert pressure over friendly and less friendly countries and a long-term strategy to shape their internal politics in certain directions—but it is based on a fundamentally different worldview. Modern liberalism of the kind exemplified by the American republic is neutral and mechanic. Its constitution is meant to be a system of checks and balances, capable of counteracting the follies of leaders through institutional and legal constraints. Its political and legal culture is deliberately neutral, keeping as much distance as possible from every particular vision of the good life. Everyone is entitled to the pursuit of happiness and, more importantly, to define on his or her own terms what happiness is. In the relations between countries, the focus is on rules and contracts. Ritual is downplayed or ignored, seen as a relic from the past.

The Chinese Tianxia is different. It emphasizes "togetherness," a complex network of ties between countries. They are much more substantial than mere legal ties. Virtues are regularly invoked: countries have relations of dependence, generosity, gratitude, respect and retribution. Relations between countries are much more difficult to navigate. Ritual is important, and so is history. Nations are better seen as intersecting stories and power the ability to determine where the story goes next.

"Togetherness" will also mean that social and economic change can be more effectively obtained. Western political societies are fragmented and diverse, with social forces moving in different directions, often resulting in a noisy and agitated state of paralysis. What China has created within its borders and what it intends to project on a larger stage is a precise and coordinated movement in predetermined directions. Opposing forces are coopted or eliminated for the sake of quick and dramatic results. Technology and success are almost synonymous. Whereas Great Britain took 154 years to double industrial output per person and the United States fifty-three years, China and India have taken just twelve and sixteen years respectively, and they have both done it on a much larger scale, with one billion people rather than 10 million. The Chinese made fifty times more mobile payments in 2016 than US consumers, trebling to $5.5 trillion in China while US payments only grew 39 per cent, to $112 billion.[40] China's Tianxia will be one of fast economic and social change, much more at ease with its costs than Western societies at present. Visions of the future will be its main currency and symbols of distinction.

Finally, the Chinese Tianxia will break with the Western model by moving decisively away from Enlightenment ideals of transparency and public knowledge. Even in its formative stage the Belt and Road is an exercise in the opacity of power. There is an exoteric doctrine of the initiative and then an esoteric practice where deals are agreed upon, often with no written evidence, and where hierarchy resembles that of security-clearance levels of access. Some of the participants know only the broadest strokes of the plan, sufficient to defend it and to communicate with lower levels, others know nothing and only a few can see months or years in advance. Or, as you sometimes hear in Beijing, just as every individual has a right to privacy, the Party also has a right to privacy. The Belt and Road is like holy writ—never revealed completely and all at once, but only bit by bit and over many decades.

We have embarked and it is almost certainly too late to go back. The world after the Belt and Road awaits us, like a new continent at the end of a long journey. It will be a world of saints, soothsayers and spooks.

NOTES

PREFACE TO THE PAPERBACK EDITION

1. Chris Buckley, "'Clean Up This Mess': The Chinese Thinkers Behind Xi's Hard Line," New York Times, August 2, 2020.

1. WHAT IS THE BELT AND ROAD?

1. Jack Farchy, "New Silk Road Will Transport Laptops and Frozen Chicken," *Financial Times*, May 9, 2016.
2. Howard French, *Everything Under the Heavens* (Knopf, 2017), p. 120.
3. John Garver, *China's Quest: The History of the Foreign Relations of the People's Republic of China* (Oxford University Press, 2016), p. 403.
4. Ezra Vogel, *Deng Xiaoping and the Transformation of China* (Harvard University Press, 2013), p. 89.
5. Wang Jisi, "China's Search for a Grand Strategy: A Rising Great Power Finds Its Way," *Foreign Affairs*, March/April 2011, pp. 68–79.
6. "Facing the Risks of the 'Going Out Strategy,'" European Council on Foreign Relations, January 2012.
7. Xu Jin and Du Zheyuan, "The Dominant Thinking Sets in Chinese Foreign Policy Research: A Criticism," *The Chinese Journal of International Politics*, September 2015, pp. 251–279.
8. "China's overcapacity crisis can spur growth through overseas expansion," *South China Morning Post*, January 7, 2014.
9. Wang Yiwei, *The Belt and Road Initiative* (New World Press, 2016), p. 4.
10. Devin Thorne and Ben Spevack, "Harbored Ambitions: How China's

Port Investments Are Strategically Reshaping the Indo-Pacific", C4ADS, 2017, pp. 16–17.

11. Mei Xinyu, "The Gwadar Port Disillusion," *Caijing*, December 19, 2016.

12. Nadège Rolland, *China's Eurasian Century? Political and Strategic Implications of the Belt and Road Initiative* (National Bureau of Asian Research, 2017), p. 113.

13. Bruno Maçães, "Russia's New Energy Gamble," *Cairo Review*, 2018.

14. Nadine Godehardt, "No End of History: A Chinese Alternative Concept of International Order", SWP Research Paper, Berlin, January 2016.

15. Wang Yiwei, *The Belt and Road Initiative: What China Will Offer the World in Its Rise* (New World Press, 2016), p. 1.

16. See Zhao Tingyang, "Rethinking Empire from a Chinese Concept 'All-under-Heaven' (Tian-xia, 天下)," *Social Identities*, January 2006, pp. 29–41.

17. "一带一路": 人类命运共同体的重要实践路径 作者: 张耀军 来源: 人民论坛

18. "China to establish court for OBOR disputes," *Asia Times*, January 25, 2018.

19. William Callahan, "China's 'Asia Dream': The Belt and Road Initiative and the New Regional Order," *Journal of Comparative Politics*, 2016, pp. 226–243.

20. 明浩, "一带一路"与"人类命运共同体, 中央民族大学学报 哲学社会科学版, 2015, p. 29.

21. Wang Jisi, "China in the Middle," *The American Interest*, 2015.

22. Dingding Chen and Jianwei Wang, "Lying Low No More? China's New Thinking on the Tao Guang Yang Hui Strategy," *China*, 2011.

23. 徐进, 郭楚, "命运共同体"概念辨析" 2017 年02期 目录.

24. Peter Harrell, Elizabeth Rosenberg and Edoardo Saravalle, "China's Use of Coercive Economic Measures," *CNAS*, June 2018.

25. Astrid Nordin, "Futures Beyond the West? Autoimmunity in China's Harmonious World", *Review of International Studies*, 2016, p. 169.

2. NUTS AND BOLTS

1. Haig Patapan & Yi Wang, "The Hidden Ruler: Wang Huning and the

Making of Contemporary China," *Journal of Contemporary China*, 2017, p. 14.

2. Astrid Nordin and Mikael Weissmann, "Will Trump make China great again? The belt and road initiative and international order," *International Affairs*, 2018, p. 237.

3. M. Dian and S. Menegazzi, *New Regional Initiatives in China's Foreign Policy* (Palgrave, 2018), p. 77.

4. Linsey Chutel, "China is exporting facial recognition software to Africa, expanding its vast database," *Quartz*, May 25, 2018.

5. "China Exim Bank Boosts Lending to Belt and Road Projects," Xinhua, January 14, 2016,

6. Wang Yingyao, "The Rise of the 'Shareholding State': Financialization of Economic Management in China'", *Socio-Economic Review*, 2015, p. 603.

7. "Building the Belt and Road: Concept, Practice and China's Contribution," Office of the Leading Group for the Belt and Road Initiative, May 2017, pp. 9–10.

8. Hasaan Khawar, "CPEC: transport or economic corridor?," *The Express Tribune*, June 5, 2018.

9. "Adhering to the Planning, Orderly and Pragmatically Build the 'Belt and Road' The Belt and Road Progress Report," The Belt and Road Progress Research Team, Renmin University of China, September 26, 2016, pp. 12–14.

10. "Seeking Belt buckle role, Kazakhstan launches China-backed financial hub," Reuters, July 5, 2018.

11. Li Lifan, "The Challenges Facing Russian-Chinese Efforts to 'Dock' the Eurasian Economic Union (EEU) and One Belt, One Road (OBOR)," *Russian Analytical Digest*, May 3, 2016.

12. Andrew Small, "First Movement, Pakistan and the Belt and Road Initiative," *Asia Policy*, 2017, p. 82.

13. Eileen Guo, "Now on Netflix: A love song to China's Belt and Road Initiative," SupChina, June 8, 2018.

14. Long Term Plan for China-Pakistan Economic Corridor (2017–2030), p. 5.

15. Faseeh Mangi, "China's Vast Intercontinental Building Plan Is Gaining Momentum," Bloomberg, April 9, 2018.

16. Murtaza Ali Shah, "Chinese company to invest $500m in Gwadar to build homes," *The News*, October 20, 2017.

17. David Brewster, "The MSRI and the Evolving Naval Balance in the Indian Ocean," in Jean-Marc F. Blanchard (ed.), *China's Maritime Silk Road Initiative and South Asia: A Political Economic Analysis of Its Purposes, Perils, and Promise* (Palgrave, 2018).

18. Shawn W. Crispin, "A man, a plan, a canal...Thailand?," *Asian Times*, January 25, 2018.

19. Chief of Naval Operations, The United States Navy Arctic Roadmap for 2014 to 2030, February 2014.

20. "Investors feel more 'assured, confident' by presence of China's base in Djibouti," *Global Times*, July 6, 2018.

21. Chi-Kong Lai, "Li Hung-chang and Modern Enterprise: The China Merchants' Company, 1872–1885," *Chinese Studies in History*, 1991, p. 41.

22. Hidetaka Yoshimatsu, "China, Japan and the South China Sea Dispute: Pursuing Strategic Goals Through Economic and Institutional Means," *Journal of Asian Security and International Affairs*, 2017, pp. 294–315.

23. Chien-peng Chung and Thomas J. Voon, "China's Maritime Silk Road Initiative: Political-Economic Calculations of Southeast Asian States", *Asian Survey*, 2017, p. 422.

24. 印度洋海权格局与中国海权的印度洋拓展，《太平洋学报》2014年5期 作者: 李剑 陈文文 金晶.

3. THE BELT AND ROAD AND THE WORLD ECONOMY

1. Richard Baldwin, *The Great Convergence: Information Technology and the New Globalization* (Harvard University Press, 2016), p. 161.

2. Kenneth Rogoff, "Will China Really Supplant US Economic Hegemony?," *Project Syndicate*, April 2, 2008.

3. Wang Jisi, "North, South, East, and West—China is in the 'Middle': A Geostrategic Chessboard," *China International Strategy Review*, p. 39.

4. *Interconnected Economies: Benefiting from Global Value Chains*, OECD, 2013.

5. Baldwin, *The Great Convergence*, p. 146.

6. "There's a Global Race to Control Batteries—and China Is Winning," *Wall Street Journal*, February 11, 2018.

7. Matthew Dalton and Lingling Wei, "How China Skirts America's Antidumping Tariffs on Steel," *Wall Street Journal*, June 4, 2018.

8. "The Fundamental Path to Accelerating the Advancement of the Building of an Internet Power" (加快推进网络强国建设的根本遵循), *Guangming Daily*, May 7, 2018.

9. 中国制造 2025, State Council, July 7, 2015.

10. Guiding Opinion on Promoting International Industrial Capacity and Equipment Manufacturing Cooperation (State Council, Guo Fa [2015] No. 30, issued May 13, 2015).

11. Guiding Opinion on Further Guiding and Standardizing the Direction of Foreign Investment, preamble (NDRC, MOFCOM, PBOC, Ministry of Foreign Affairs, Guo Ban Fa [2017] No. 74, issued Aug. 4, 2017).

12. "China Manufacturing 2025," European Union Chamber of Commerce in China, 2017, p. 51.

13. "Germany Vetoes Chinese Purchase of Business Citing Security Grounds," *Wall Street Journal*, July 26, 2018.

14. James McGregor, *China's Drive for 'Indigenous Innovation': A Web of Industrial Policies*, Washington, DC: U.S. Chamber of Commerce, 2010.

15. Andrew Polk, "China Is Quietly Setting Global Standards," Bloomberg, May 6, 2018.

16. Noah Barkin, "'Boiled frog syndrome': Germany's China problem", Reuters, April 15, 2018.

17. President Trump Announces Strong Actions to Address China's Unfair Trade, Press Release, Office of the United States Trade Representative, March, 2018.

18. Minxin Pei, "Xi risks losing face in a trade war with Trump," *Nikkei Asian Review*, July 9, 2018

19. Olaf Merk, "Geopolitics and commercial seaports," *RIS*, Fall 2017, p. 74.

20. Qiushi Feng, *Variety of Development: Chinese Automakers in Market Reform and Globalization* (Palgrave, 2018).

21. 胡怀邦: 以开发性金融服务"一带一路"战略 胡怀邦: 以开发性金融服务"一带一路"战略.

22. 金琦董事长在"一带一路"高峰论坛的午餐演讲.

23. "Long-Term Plan on China-Pakistan Economic Corridor," National Development and Reform Commission (NDRC), P.R.C. China Development Bank (CDB), December 2015.

24. Tristan Kenderdine, "China's industrial capacity policy is a one-way street," *South China Morning Post*, June 8, 2017

4. THE BELT AND ROAD AND WORLD POLITICS

1. 中巴经济走廊实地调研报告, pp. 28–29.

2. Jichang Lulu, "State-managed Buddhism and Chinese-Mongolian relations," China Policy Institute: Analysis, June 23, 2017.

3. Raja Mohan, *Samudra Manthan: Sino-Indian Rivalry in the Indo-Pacific* (Brookings Institution Press, 2012).

4. Bob Carr, "The shrinking 'Quad': how the alliance is going nowhere as Japan and India court China," *South China Morning Post*, May 17, 2018.

5. Josh Rogin, "Trump's Indo-Pacific strategy: Where's the beef?", *Washington Post*, June 6, 2018

6. "Trump rants behind closed doors with CEOs" Politico, August 8, 2018.

7. "Investment in Indonesia's Sabang port will be test of India's diplomatic wisdom," *Global Times*, June 28, 2018.

8. Jonathan Hillman, "The clouds gathering around China's Belt and Road," *Nikkei Asian Review*, May 16, 2018.

9. Raffaello Pantucci, "China's South Asian Miscalculation," *Current History*, April 2018, p. 147.

10. Andrey Kortunov, "Indo-Pacific or Community of Common Destiny?" Russian International Affairs Council, May 28, 2018.

11. "Absorb and Conquer: An EU Approach to Russian and Chinese Integration in Eurasia", European Council on Foreign Relations, 2016.

12. Nicolas Moës, "Is it a Transatlantic, Transpacific or Eurasian global economy?" *Bruegel*, February 14, 2018.

13. François Godement and Abigaël Vasselier, "China at the Gates: A New Power Audit of EU-China Relations", European Council of Foreign Relations, 2017, p. 90.

14. Thorsten Benner et al., "Authoritarian Advance: Responding to China's Growing Political Influence in Europe", GPPI, February 2018, p. 16.

15. "EU sets collision course with China over 'Silk Road' rail project," *Financial Times*, February 20, 2017.

16. "China's Silk Road Initiative Sows European Discomfort," *Wall Street Journal*, May 15, 2017.

17. See "Balancing China," *Asia Policy Brief*, Bertelsmann Stiftung, May 3, 2018.

5. THE WORLD AFTER THE BELT AND ROAD

1. An earlier version of this section was published in *Politico Europe* in July 2018.

2. "China scales back investment in Ethiopia," *Financial Times*, June 3, 2018.

3. Will Doig, *High-Speed Empire: Chinese Expansion and the Future of Southeast Asia* (Colombia Global Reports, 2018). See also Tom Miller, *China's Asian Dream: Empire Building Along the New Silk Road* (Zed Books, 2017).

4. "China emerges as wild card in elections across Asia," *Nikkei Asian Review*, June 5, 2008.

5. "China's Xi offers fresh $295 million grant to Sri Lanka," Reuters, July 22, 2018.

6. Jeremy Page and Saeed Shah, "China's Global Building Spree Runs Into Trouble in Pakistan," *Wall Street Journal*, July 22, 2018. "Pakistan turns to China to avoid foreign currency crisis," *Financial Times*, May 23, 2018.

7. Andrew Small, "Buyer's Remorse: Pakistan's Elections and the Precarious Future of the China-Pakistan Economic Corridor," War on the Rocks, July 27, 2018.

8. "China needs to act as a responsible creditor," *Financial Times*, April 29, 2018.

9. Andrew Nathan, "The Chinese World Order," *New York Review of Books*, October 12, 2017.

10. "China development banks expand links with foreign lenders," *Financial Times*, July 15, 2018.

11. Brahma Chellaney, "China's Debt-Trap Diplomacy," Project Syndicate, January 23, 2017.

12. Imminent Fears, Immediate Hopes, 我們當下的恐懼與期待, Xu Zhangrun 許章潤. Translated with commentary and notes by Geremie R. Barmé, China Heritage.

13. "Xi behind coercive tactics in East China Sea: documents," *Japan Times*, December 2, 2017.

14. Oliver Stuenkel, *Post-Western World* (Polity, 2016), p. 156.

15. Kevin G. Cai, "The One Belt One Road and the Asian Infrastructure Investment Bank: Beijing's New Strategy of Geoeconomics and Geopolitics," *Journal of Contemporary China*, 2018.

16. "The 'American century' has come to its end," *Global Times*, August 20, 2017.

17. G. John Ikenberry (ed.), *Power, Order, and Change in World Politics* (Cambridge University Press, 2014), p. 106.

18. "EU ambassadors band together against Silk Road," *Handelsblatt*, April 17, 2008

19. "Sharp Power: Rising Authoritarian Influence," International Forum for Democratic Studies, 2017

20. Richard Fontaine and Daniel Kliman, "On China's New Silk Road, Democracy Pays A Toll," *Foreign Policy*, May 16, 2018.

21. 人民日报：推动构建人类命运共同体, 2017年11月19日05:04.

22. "How the Belt and Road Project Fills a Global Governance Vacuum," *Sixth Tone*, November 12, 2017.

23. Angela Stanzel, "Fear and loathing on the New Silk Road: Chinese security in Afghanistan and beyond," July 2018, ECFR/264.

24. Branko Milanovic, "The west is mired in 'soft' development. China is trying the 'hard' stuff," *The Guardian*, May 17, 2017.

25. 国务院办公厅转发 商务部等部门关于扩大进口 促进对外贸易平衡发展意见的通知 国办, 2018, 53 号.

26. Michael Schuman, "China's Global Ambitions Could Split the World Economy," Bloomberg, October 26, 2017.

27. Thomas Wright, *All Measures Short of War: The Contest for the 21st Century and the Future of American Power* (Yale University Press, 2017), p. 1.

28. Aaron L. Friedberg, "Competing with China," *Survival*, May 2018.

29. David Autor, David Horn and Gordon Hanson, "The China Shock: Learning from Labor Market Adjustment to Large Changes in Trade," NBER Working Paper, January 2016.

30. Michael Mann, *The China Fantasy* (Viking, 2007).

31. François Godement and Abigael Vasselier, *China at the Gates: A New Power Audito of EU-China Relations* (ECFR, 2017).

32. *National Security Strategy of the United States of America* (December 2017), p. 17.

33. Ibid., 25.

34. Jinghan Zeng, "China declares ideological war," *Policy Forum*, November 3, 2017.

35. Zhang Weiwei, *The China Horizon: Glory and Dream of a Civilizational State* (World Century, 2016).

36. Jiang Shigong, "Philosophy and History: Interpreting the 'Xi Jinping Era' through Xi's Report to the Nineteenth National Congress of the CCP," *The China Story*, May 11, 2018. Originally published in 开放时代.

37. Nadège Rolland, *China's Eurasian Century: Political and Strategic Implications of the Belt and Road Initiative* (The National Bureau of Asian Research, 2017), pp. 143–44.

38. Jonathan Holslag, *China's Coming War with Asia* (Polity, 2015).

39. "Xi's world order: July 2024," *The Economist*, July 7, 2018.

40. Hugh Peyman, *China's Change: The Greatest Show on Earth* (World Scientific, 2018).

INDEX

INDEX

INDEX

INDEX

INDEX

INDEX

INDEX

INDEX

INDEX

INDEX

INDEX

INDEX

INDEX

INDEX

INDEX

INDEX

INDEX

INDEX